DOWN A COBB

Kathleen Panettieri

LITORIA PRESS

© Copyright 2021. Kathleen Panettieri.
Title: Down a Cobblestone Lane
ISBN: 978-0-6451145-6-0 (paperback)
Subject: Australian Poetry
Published by: Litoria Press (a Division of Wordsmart Enterprises)
litoriapress@gmail.com
+61 3 5985 2112

Cover Design: Deanna Defina
Internal images created using Pixabay vector graphics

A catalogue record for this work is available from the National Library of Australia

Applause

"Kathleen employs language to articulate what one can only feel… empathy, through writing, is her true gift.

Using poignant imagery Kathleen takes us on a visceral exploration of identity, place, the wounds of migration and resilience. *Down a cobblestone lane* is a collection I will immerse myself in, again and again."

~*Mary Chydiriotis*

"There is such a visual, rich depth of thought woven into Kathleen's poetry; it is about endurance and heartfelt hope on her life journey, about the reality of what life is and can be if we believe in our own inner strength."

~*Dinka Bednjacic*

"Kathleen's *Down a Cobblestone Lane* journeys with detail into memories and moments of a rich Greek and Irish heritage.

It is a generous and often tender book filled with poetic voice that truly is the spirit of Goliath, championing her battles with a love of life.

We are all better for reading it."

~*Fotoula Reynolds* - poet and author of *The Sanctuary of my Garden*, *Silhouettes* and *Along the Macadam Road*.

Foreword

The poetry world is large, as I have found out over the last four years. It is difficult to stand out in the crowd when there is such an array of talent on display, whether it is found on social media, heard at poetry events, or read in journals, magazines, and other publications.

Nonetheless, Kathleen Panettieri's work did indeed stand out — her poems are poignant and elegant, providing insights and wisdom that address very real issues. Personal yet universal, these well-crafted lines make sense, without ever becoming didactic.

So, while I was starting up Litoria Press in early 2021, I was quick to ask Kathleen if I could publish some of her poems in a book. As you can see, she agreed!

I love the way Kathleen's work represents a multifaceted, expansive life; a life that reflects her Greek-Irish heritage, growing up in Australia, a life of connection with family, of discovery and growth. Along the cobblestone lane we find struggles, re-examinations, and a redefinition of spirituality and what it means to be alive.

I hope you enjoy reading this book as much as I enjoyed making it. I invite you to join Kathleen in her celebration of life.

Julia Kaylock, poet, editor and publisher.

Acknowledgments

Heartfelt thanks to my niece, Deanna Defina for the beautiful cover design.

Much gratitude to Julia Kaylock for her publishing work and for making it so easy for me to make this book a reality.

I dedicate this book to my dear parents
Nick Goulas and Eileen Hamilton

Come join me as I continue the journey I began with my first volume of poetry, *Trails of Light*. With this book, I venture *Down a Cobblestone Lane* gathering memories and reflections. Images past and present are developed as 'Snapshots from a dark room'; the big questions stretch across the generations in 'Readings from the book of answers'. 'Threading the rosary' is my prayerful tribute to life, in which our being is one essential and continuing creation.

May the lanterns of love guide you on your journey.

Tribute

Diagnosed with cancer in 2016, I began a different kind of journey, taking me back into my past to rescue poetry I had written over the previous thirty years and publish my first book *Trails of Light* in 2018.

Poetry has continued to be my bastion of strength producing the bulk of poems in this book, written over the last three years.

My poem 'Goliath and I' on the opposite page is a tribute to all the medical practitioners and nurses who have been my accompanying angels on this journey.

Goliath and I

Into the scanner
Be still be silent
In a machine's embrace
Let its mechanical eye
Stare into my depths
Let it see
What skin and flesh hide
All that lies inside
Whisper my mantras
Into the silence of my mind
Into the eye of my Goliath
I have done battle with my
Small armoury fine hands
Of the surgeon sharp steel scalpels
The killer rays select poisons
Let comfort find this small creature

How many times?
How many times must I hurl
These stones of wrath at the giant?
As the eye moves around
Coldly clinically observing
Beneath my protective veils
Is the treatment still working?

*

All clear.....Goliath still down for the count.....Hallelujah!!!
   ...2018, 2019, 2020, 2021

x

Contents

Down a cobblestone lane   *1*

Ruby   *2*

Ghost house   *4*

Silhouettes on a dusty street   *5*

Dark moon waiting   *6*

Readings from the book of answers   *8*

Redemption   *11*

Partly truth, mostly fiction   *12*

Snap-shots from a dark room   *14*

Touching Centre   *16*

Colossus unveiled   *18*

A modern fairy tale   *20*

Streets that knew my name   *22*

O pateras mou (My father)   *23*

Seamless   *24*

Ruins   *25*

Under the tree   *26*

Distortions in the mirror   *28*

That silver bird   *29*

Red heart   *30*

Woman   *32*

Draughtsperson   *33*

Show me your colour   *34*

Threading the rosary   *36*

Dust dreams   *38*

Lady Quixote   *39*

Reading Sylvia Plath   *40*

Port of Messina   *42*

An unknown hero   *44*

The cry of the dust   *45*

Where wild oats grow   *46*

Burning   *48*

Like, living   *50*

Bucephalus   52
A river of words   54
Divergent   56
This earthenware vessel   57
After the storm   58
Fracture   59
Like Alice   60
The ringing of the bell   61
A parting gift   62
Decidious   63
Lanterns   64
Overture   66
Where wizards play   68
Under a gypsy moon   70
The face of dilemma   72
Ancestry   73
A place called home   74
Out of emptiness   76
Shadows and lies   77
Myths of paradise   78
Polarities   81
The constant garden   82
Out of Eden   84
Undone   86
Burning pages   88
The Way   90
At the intersection   91
Inside my box of shadows   92
Boxed in   93
Heartbeat   94
Uriel rising   96
Burning up the night   97
Utopia   98
The lion and the lamb   100
Tightrope   101
Resting place   102
Yesterday's ghosts   103

The appointed time	104
Undercover lover	105
Walking on water	106
Caprice	107
Finite	108
Strange bedfellows	109
Resurrection	110
Wood smoke signals	112
Mirror eyes	114
Disturbed	115
A la carte	116
The virtuoso	118
Makeshift Living	119
Two Step	120
On Chelsea sidewalk	121
Unmasked	122
This thing called love	124
Hurts	126
Jericho falling	127
Law of attraction	128
As dead trees fall	130
Mother and child	132
Mercy	134
The trial of error	136
Between the beats	138
The Land of True	139
Language of the night	140
Wounded bird	142
One morning in Eden	143
Casualty of war	144
The silent deep	145
Crucifixion	146
Night bird	147
Spirit of place	148
Wind song	150
Easy like a warm spring day	152
Never enough	153

Clouds and rainbows 154
Family portrait 155
A sensible choice 156
Now rider 158
On dragon-fly wings 159
Winter haiku 160
Lament of the unreturned soldier 162
Movement in two parts 164
Café blues 166
Tear down your walls 167
Mea Culpa 168
Universal child 170
The anguish of Pierrot 172
Epilogue 174
Bazaar of abandoned things 176
Melancholy 178
A street called one way 180
That primal cry 182
Firewall 184
At the slip of your foot 187
Deep pockets 188
Star crossed 189
Dreamers 190
Earth dance 192
Ticket for the ride 193
La rinascente 194

Acknowledgement

'Dust dreams' (p.38) was first published in Mar 2020 edition of *The Writers and Readers Magazine*

Down a cobblestone lane

Down the lane
Over uneven cobblestones
Over the rickety bridge
Leading me back
And I am shrinking
Smaller and smaller
My hand barely reaching
The handrail, my feet
Wearing small shoes again
And I am still her, the one
Who inhabited my childhood
Just like Alice, I push my way
In through the back gate
Into that old wonderland
Past the old wood shed
The sheets flapping on the line
Past windows that still
Recognise my face, a ghostly
Blur peering in at darkness
I am sitting on the back step
Barely able to talk, calling
In my baby voice
"Open the door, open the door!"
But the walls are deaf and blind
They shimmer, receding now,
Out of reach, leaving me behind
The past has closed its door
Nothing is as it was before
Just memory playing those
Old old tricks once more.

Ruby

I remember being there
in the sitting room with them
my mother and her friend Ruby
from down the street
Ruby with the long red hair
like Rita Hayworth
I am sitting on the sofa
as though I'm not there
my little girl legs and feet
too short to touch the floor
My mummy isn't herself anymore
she is someone I don't know
and music is playing
on our shiny new radiogram
I want to reach out and touch
that beautiful long red hair
swinging around Ruby dancing
talking and laughing out loud
as the record is spinning around
and Lily Pons is singing in our room
in a voice high enough
to touch mountain tops
I hear my mother's voice
bursting from her throat to reach
the very highest notes, too,
as they dance and are happy
Ruby and my mother

KATHLEEN PANETTIERI

And I am stuck in a solitary place
inside my skin and bones
watching them and all I know
is that I want to have
Ruby's long red hair
and be a part of whatever
it is that they share.

Ghost house

Driving past the old house
That belonged to an aunt and uncle
Long gone, I summon up all the ghosts
Who raise their heads as I go
Past. The Christmases and lost
Cousins, aunties, uncles who
All gathered there when the
House was still young and we and
The world, still small. All gone
Because families have grown
Too large, too far spread.
But the dead remember, I feel
It every time that I drive past.
The old walls shift a little then
Settle back again and I feel
A tingle in my spine. It happens
Every time I pass, like a gasp
Of breath or a sudden draft
Springing up to reach me from
Hands that have long gone away.
The old walls have a new coat
Of paint now and modern touches
Have been added, keeping up with
Trendy town houses, mushrooms
that have sprung up all around.
But it is still an old house among
New ones and the ghosts have
Kept their old address and cling
Tightly to the walls within walls.

KATHLEEN PANETTIERI

Silhouettes on a dusty street

Now and then we remember when
We were playing out on an empty street
Running through the creaking old rusty gate
Feeling the freedom of our bare-skinned feet
On that old familiar dusty street
Riding the red metal scooter with its clackety wheels
Bare feet skidding on the burning road
Deaf to the hounds of time snapping at our heels
The roar of the future snarling on impatient wheels
Now and then we remember when
The days were long and the pace was placid
On that dusty road where children gathered
The wind swirling dirt on our bare-skinned feet
The evening weaving its shadows over our patchwork games
Before time clanged shut that old rusty gate and
Burned our silhouettes onto that dusty street.

Dark moon waiting

A storm rages somewhere
Bringing down darkness
There is always another storm
Somewhere
Belligerent, bullying
Throwing hearts around
Like broken branches
It will pass, storms always pass
Like temper tantrums shaking off
An infinity of aftermath
Leaving tangled roots
Unwilling to unravel
Futures savaged by pasts

There is a house somewhere
Wearing a picket fence disguise
Lending its backdrop to malevolence
Holding smudged images of
Haunted eyes staring into a mirror
Of baleful obscurity
Behind windows that don't speak
Usually there are children twisted and
Left un-staked on shaky ground
Soft pillows whipped from under them
By hands leaked of trust
Leaving blood ice-cold behind
The beguile of soft lies

KATHLEEN PANETTIERI

There is always a weary sun rising
On foreboding
Dark moon waiting
Lending shadow to menace
Love's hand poised cathartic
Behind the unseen light in other eyes
Always waiting on the other side of storms.

Readings from the book of answers

For Sinead

When I was a young grandmother
I was asked a question
by my three year old granddaughter
It was probably the most important
question I have ever been asked.
How do you answer, in a way
that a three year old can understand,
The question that the greatest
minds still wrestle with?
In a plaintive little voice, she asked
"Grandma, what is life?"
I thought long and hard, then
answered her
"Life means.....that you are here
and that you can do things"

How could I tell her then, that her
being here placed her at the centre
of everything and that her doing
sent ripples across the vastness of infinity

And that light pours itself down from the heavens
in a constant stream that never stops
and can never stop
and each image cast upon that light
will find its reflection upon the earth

And everything was created equal
with its own eyes to see
ears to hear and be a part of the
whole of everything
to record it all a book with endless
pages was given
to be held in the vastness of eternity

So to this avail does the elephant
cede its might to lie down in its pool of ivory
another elephant will take its place
and another and another will share
its birth

All will be of light and its constancy to prevail
each day the first and last, each night
to rise from the turning light
you and I, the first equation, will dance
the remnants of night away
rise as we rose with the first sun to
burn and own the day

The oyster expires in the throes of its friction
creating the pearl that will weep from a crown
each disguise that is worn to slowly
fade and be torn
each clown its purpose in the circus of life

Moonlight will keep dying, bleeding its dreams away
and falling stars bequeath their light
to the darkness of night
the earth will gather up the seeds
that time did borrow
to soak deep deep down into its own furrows

Bodies will sweat and strive before
they give up the ghost
to the huge blank page waiting
eager to contain its own potential
you and I shall keep dancing on as
old worlds fade to dust
to let a new world rise, as rise it always must

And it was written and will always be written
Every question will be heard and will
have its answer
Yes, I have watched my granddaughter growing
and there she is
running with her arms full of dreams
across the precious page unfolding
I have heard her song of joy as
each dream spread itself out over the years
in a riot of colours around her
doing what it takes to make a
dream come true
being the answer to her own question.

KATHLEEN PANETTIERI

Redemption

When I close my eyes
They come whispering in my dreams

I can imagine them all
Waving and watching intently

Hidden by a cumulus of past lives
Beyond that invisible shore

Chattering amongst themselves
Nodding or shaking their heads

Calculating into a repentant algebra
The sums of their inheritance

Watching what I have done
With threads they have bequeathed

While I tend their unhealed wounds
Gathering, sewing and binding

All that remained unforgiven
Into a banner of weeping stars

To hang against the darkling sky
Heralding some kind of redemption.

Partly truth, mostly fiction

I remember meeting you
Once before, in a story I heard

Or in a book somewhere
You wore another face then

Called yourself by a different name
Now you sit at this table

On this avenue, at this rendezvous,
Sipping your black coffee

And spilling bitter words
All over my open pages

"I thought I loved you"
Falling out of your mouth

"But I changed my mind"
Puffing on your cigarette

Pages going up in smoke
And I am stupidly crying as

I stumble from the table past
Strangers at other tables

Removing my fictional face
From another unhappy ending

KATHLEEN PANETTIERI

I foolishly believed that love
Was an affair of the heart

I erase myself from another
Book of blank pages with

Love's thorns punctuating
A crazy dialogue in my head

And its wilted petals scattered
In a confusion of fading promises

Around my aching heart
I leave you at an empty table

Wearing your stranger's face
Like any other closed book.

Snap-shots from a dark room

Northern Ireland 1920s

Great gulps of air threaten
To burst my lungs, choking
The screams in my throat
Wearing my Mother's skin
I am looking through
Her little-girl eyes
Listening with her
Shell-shocked ears
"Your Da is dead!"
Black words bleeding onto
A bleak future "They shot him!"
Crunched out through clenched teeth
He took the bullet that tore
Through her innocent heart
A light went out leaving
Its harsh negative image
Trapped in a dark room
And we, swaddled in her history,
Weaned from her bitter-sweet milk
Onto Troubles that refused to end

*

KATHLEEN PANETTIERI

Northern Greece 1940s

A letter arrives
Finding its way across oceans
Separating him from family
Carrying black words scrawled
On numbing white paper
My father's hands
Must have trembled
His face must have crumbled
As he read news
Of his father's disappearance
Betrayed into enemy hands
In his war-torn country
He never spoke of it to us
Digested his solitary
Meal of grief. Shed lone tears
In his own dark room
His father never
Returned home
We never knew
What we had lost

*

Their black and white negatives
developed into
The multi-coloured coat I now wear

Touching Centre

The river rages like an angry bull
I feel the pull of a capricious tide

The river drags me down into
Its stormy rapids ride

Past coagulated hornet's nests
Of intrigue and terror floating free

I smell the rising odour of fear
I want to close my eyes and hide

In the depths of this hallowed moment
Lying deep below the tide

I turn away from the madness and
Confusion that blights the world

Reach out to the deep heart of love
Feel its arms wrapped tight around me

Breathe in the essence of a depthless purity
That whispers of endless being

Where I am at the centre and circumference
Of all that rages there

Where my heart can touch the anchor
Of hidden grace that lives within

KATHLEEN PANETTIERI

Dissolving fleeting apparitions of
Ghostly flotsam that linger still

Releasing my harrowed heart to be its own
Mathematician and the barometer

Of my changing days. So I may ride
On waves of gratitude into this

Effervescent living river
With its tempests and its tides

Colossus unveiled

Midnight in my resting garden
With its muted shades of black and grey
The witching hour with all
The little night creatures
Rustling through invisibility
Pricking up their ears
As I wade through grass
Stripped of all colour
Embraced by deep swathes
As mysterious as love, I can sense
A dark immensity watching me
From my portal into infinity
Speaking to me in a language
I once understood
Along the edges of the bay
I can picture little moored boats
Dipping and swaying with
Waving ribbons of moonlight
Moved by the passage of this
Invisible colossus with its
Language of deep rhythms
Waves and pulses echoing in
Beating heart, surging blood

KATHLEEN PANETTIERI

Unveiled, the colossus has cast
its star-spangled cape
Across black velvet skies
And conjured away the light
Leaving a thin crescent of yellow
Moon suspended on the whole of Everything.
Needing no words
Its brooding presence owns
The deep space of stillness

I breathe in its vital sustenance
Knowing that dawn will restore to me
The helm of the day where I may
Pluck from sibilant streams of sound
Tentative words and weave my
Nets to capture edges and
Dimensions of felt images
Gifts to place at its feet.

A modern fairy tale

Wearing a Cinderella dress
walking in Cinderella shoes,
finding the way home by midnight.
Never, ever speak to a stranger
there's danger out on the streets.

One, two, buckle my shoe
only speak if you're spoken to.

Three, four, wait outside the door
never, ever, ask for more.

Fairy tales, fairy tales, fed on
myths and outworn fables
dished up onto their tables.
Modern life can turn to ashes
too many of a young girl's dreams.

Five, six, picking up sticks
light the fire, put the kettle on the hob,

learn to become a Superwoman.
Go out and find that perfect job
keep chasing that outworn dream.
It really is quite alarming
maybe there is no Prince Charming.

Seven, eight, who knows what lies
waiting behind the swinging gate.

Nine, ten, just a big fat hen
no goose laying her golden egg.

Eleven, twelve, dig and delve,
never give up, never give up.

Cinderella shoes
Re-tracing their steps
Searching for the crumbs
Of happy ever after.

Streets that knew my name

Two Venetian glass swans
One red, one green, souvenirs
Of a visit to Murano long ago
Greet me each morning from
The shelf where they sit suspended
Slowly gathering the dusty veneer of living
Their delicate necks turned windwards
Following me from place to place
Houses I have lived in
Streets that knew my name
Trailing the paraphernalia of
Days, of weeks, of years
Precious clutter that still remains
And these words that spill from me
Will they shrivel on brute uncaring
Tides and fall to dust like all else
Or will they flutter like soft feathers
Carried by the wind as it hurries by
Or scraps of old torn lace clinging
To its tail and whispering of places
They have been, unforgettable
Moments suspended delicately
Like these swans silently swimming
Through waters of eternity
Along streets that knew my name.

KATHLEEN PANETTIERI

O pateras mou
(My father)

Daddy, you have been long gone
Too far away and beyond touch,
Yet the further you slip from me
The clearer I am able to see you.
The more able I am to venerate you.
So today, in your honour,
I choose to spoil myself
In these uncertain, darkened times
Of pestilence and pandemic,
Sweeping across the globe.

So, sit with me at my table,
Which I dress as an altar to your felt presence,
And share with me those delicacies
That you once loved to eat.
Crispy, tangy, Greek spanakopita.
Succulent, juicy, green honeydew melon
And we will finish with a flourish
Of good kafé, accompanied with
Your favourite of favourites,
Sweet rose-scented Turkish delight.

Then I will invite you to dance the sirtaki
And we will bravely step together,
To the strumming, plaintive and
Yearning tones of the bouzouki.
Yiasou! O pateras mou.

Seamless

Let me borrow that red rose
You keep hidden in your heart
The thorn that plunged so deep
It cut and made you bleed
Let me touch those aching fingers
Of pain that linger there
Then wash me with the waves of joy
The river saves for you
Pull me down into your undertow
Let me steal a look through your eyes
So I can feel all the things that you know

Seamless this river that flows
Timeless is its afterglow

The river runs, the river pulls
You wildly on its tides
The river runs, the river knows
The secrets that you hide
The river runs, the river winds
Through twists and turns within your mind
The river runs, the river murmurs
Its haunting yearning song
Let me steal a look through your eyes
So I can feel all the things that you know

Seamless this river that flows
Timeless is its afterglow.

KATHLEEN PANETTIERI

Ruins

us with our sticky little baby fingers
tearing open the parcels of our lives
laughing as we fill our tiny cups
with streams of steamy pretend tea
happily choosing memories from
our tiny pretty plates and crying as
passing winds spill them on the ground
while we play this game called living
you and me until now after a lifetime
we're sitting sipping our cups of grown-up tea
and passing each other our pretty plates
of forgotten delicacies that crumble
as we place them in our open eager mouths
both laughing
because you can remember the
things I never saw and I remember
those things left lying on the floor
now we're both crying as we pass
around the secrets and the lies
it is no surprise to find that things
were never as we remembered or
that any of it could last forever
the memories we saved were never
infallible or heavily cast in stone
and we chew at their crumbling
morsels of a half forgotten past to
find them fallen into a pile of ruins
leaving the bare bones of truth lying
stark in our hands and in our eyes.

Under the tree

She is not the girl
she used to be
Dreaming beneath the apple tree
Blossoms
spilling
softly
down
In lacy veils upon her head

She was just a girl
who hitched a ride
Upon a bright
and
falling
star
The world keeps
spinning and
spilling
down
In jigsaw pieces upon her head

She is not the girl
she used to be
Rising wind shakes the apple tree
The world is
spinning
upside
down
Casting cryptic shadows
all around

KATHLEEN PANETTIERI

She is climbing mountains
in her head
Softly weeping
into her silences
Her prayers of hope
for better
days
ahead

And the wind will share
with her its
promises
To dreams beneath the apple tree
Blossoms
spilling
gently
down
In lacy veils upon her bed.

Distortions in the mirror

I walk past him
Sitting on the pavement
And my legs turn to stone
For a long moment
I feel myself
In the depths of his eyes
Till I recoil
In self-defence
He blindly emanates pain
That pulls like love
And waits for a hand-out
I wonder about his home
His life, his story
The distortions in the mirror
Of himself
I drop a coin
In his outstretched hand
To salve my own disquiet
Rich man, poor man
Beggar man, thief
This man's face
Wears the shape of grief
The twisted shape
Of my squashed down fears
I walk on
In a distorted haze of tears.

KATHLEEN PANETTIERI

That silver bird

Daddy, did it break your heart?
When you waved me onto that silver bird
I never heard if you were crying too
Waving your white handkerchief in the air
Watching from the ground as it flew me away
Up into those waiting clouds
Daddy, you kept your pain inside
I never heard you speak it out loud

Children, don't listen, do they?
Children, aren't meant to listen, are they?
They need to walk out on that ledge
Hear the wind roaring under their wings
Staring straight into that empty face
At the edge of the world

Daddy, I've been crying too
Just like you, there's nothing I could do
That silver bird of freedom pulled
their hands away
One by one, I've watched them all fly away
Staring straight into that empty face
At the edge of the world

Red heart

Terra Australis

Thrum thrum thrum
Of an ancient music
Humming across the land,
Black feet throbbing on the burning ground
of the Never Never sand.
The black man's chant rising plaintive
like a prayer,
Pulsating across the dusty plains,
His boomerang whirling through the mists of time
Will never return.
Red dust swirling in a dying sun
Over the red red heart
Of a timeless land.
Red dust falling
Swirling swirling.
Lost notes calling
Rolling rolling.
Children of the spirit of this dreaming land
Calling calling,
To the ghosts still roaming in their
No man's land terra nullius

Black hands mixing the colours of the earth
Red and brown yellow and ochre.
Fingers stirring the soil to life,
Primitive shadows moving on cave walls, stained relics on
Rock faces coming alive again with
their musty smell of history.

KATHLEEN PANETTIERI

The spirit of this land weaving its
skeins of memories
Deep into the mulga scrub, into the
layers of the dusty soil.
Rainbow serpent coiled dreaming in the skies
Sheds its colours when the rain dies.
Now wayward winds have come rattling
The creaking bones of old traditions,
Spilling into an ancient womb
Vagrant seeds of new directions.
A hot dry wind with its dusty throat
Has swallowed the parched out centuries.
The wild dingo sniffs at the new blood
seeping into
The spirit of the land, the spirit of place
The spirit of its changing face,
This old land breathing its new
breaths
Under the Southern Cross.
Red heart thumping thumping
Ancient blood pumping
Into the veins of the future.

Woman

She was Scheherazade of the thousand tales
Salome dancing with her seven veils
She was Eve wandering in the garden
Of her own exquisite delight
Then feeling the night descending
Pulling the ground from beneath her feet
Becoming Alice falling falling over and over again
Staring into her own unfathomable mirror
At the interminable stains of her unfurled dreams
Nightly she coaxes the face of a secretive moon
From behind its blanket of clouds
Stares at diamonds lighting up the darkening sky
And bears the heaviness of each orphan dream
Moving in her towards its own new
And freshly emerging birth
Her arms spreading their sheltering wings
Over the face of each awakening
To a brand new earth
Each emerging heart beat stirring
In unison with hers
Because she is Woman,
The eternal doorway to every dream

KATHLEEN PANETTIERI

Draughtsperson

Forgive me
While I go back
To the drawing board
Of myself
The careless and foolish
Lines I drew
The shadows
I misconstrued
I must adjust
I confused the images
Floating in my head
Our faces overlapped
And what I saw
Was not me
Not you
I will take up the pencil
Re-draw each line
Sketch a new
Resolution
Look in the mirror
Of myself
Try to capture
The light
Try to get each angle
Right this time
I am still just
A work in progress

Show me your colour

See these brush strokes
These smudges of colour
I am a woman
And I have wept
I am a woman
And I have slept
With my own demons
And those strange others
Who have crept
From their fiery pits
To inhabit my dreams

I am a woman
And I am a mother
I have leapt into
That crucible and lived
With both sides
Of motherhood
The soft and the hard
The lean and the plenty
And the thud of empty
Show me the colour
Of your pain

I am a woman
And I have bled my girlhood
Onto this tapestry
Of living colour, this
Bitter sweet Calvary
Taking me to adulthood

KATHLEEN PANETTIERI

My once soft pliant
Hands turned granite
Hard, holding tight as
Anchors against this
Stormy sea. This is me.

I have sunk to the bottom
Of the ocean and risen
Robed in all its shades
Show me your colour
I will show you my rainbow.

Threading the rosary

I.M. Jane McGiffin

I saw a photo of her once
Sitting sedate and serene
Captured in faded sepia shades
Wearing her sixteen years
And her long blonde hair
Tied at the nape with a bow.
That was before she wed her tall fair
Policeman and before wedding bells
Turned to funeral tolls and five small children
Bequeathed to the future.
She was taught to recite from
The syllabus of prayer but
She soon learned to pray without
Stopping.
She was our Granny
The only grandparent we knew.
I remember the visits and
Boisterous happy Irish Christmases
Punctuated with her soft brogue.
She prayed a lot, fingering
Her string of beads
Bringing her own sacrificial altar
To church on Sundays.

KATHLEEN PANETTIERI

Her wedding gift to me
Was a crucifix,
She knew that road
Had travelled it twice
Bearing six more children.
So many lives, all of us candles
Burning down on her altar,
Threading us all like beads
Onto her rosary.
Digging down through the shredded
Layers of living and cultivating the soul
Love grows roses and thorns.

Dust dreams

We rise from the hearth to gather the reins
The stuff of myth and fable burns in our veins
Pierce me one more time with the sword of pain
And watch me as I bleed again
The night is a schism, our prison so long,
Tolling the notes of its mournful song
The morning will remember us as just
Falling motes drifting down to dust

I was Cinderella, you were my prince
We've been inveigled by fantasy ever since
I put on that devil-red riding hood
Lost myself in that tangled wood
Where you morphed to the wolf who devoured my heart
And tore my innocent name apart
Two dust spiders weaving our webs of intent
Both of us hanging by the threads of discontent

But we were just the stuff of dreams
Searing fingers of light tear at the seams
Of these cloaks of dark
Whisperings of ash naked and stark
The dawning light will decipher us as just
Ghostly scrawls on the fallen dust
We return to the hearthstone of the living fire
Consumed by the embers of its endless desire.

Lady Quixote

January always brings
A strange turbulence
It whirls and pulls forward
The jaded steps of December
I stand at the cliff edge
Of my own indecisions
Staring out into a wild coaxing
And challenging peace
To do and to be my own
Difference my own more
Better than everything
That has come before
I have submerged my
Misgivings under mounds
Of festive cake and chocolate
I have raised my glass to the
Implacable faces of the zodiac
Who and what could I
Not then be with tentative
Magnificent additions
And essential subtractions
What is it that each New
Year demands of myself
I rustle my acquiescence into the
Challenge of a passing wind burst
Eyes alert for omens and signs
I resolutely jump free falling
Into the quixotic wanderings
Of my own chaotic continuance

Reading Sylvia Plath

You left us your black shapes
Scrawled against an endless white
I hope you woke to light
Waiting all around
I hope it claimed you
From the ground
I hope you woke to mercy
From the ire
That did confound
A tortured mind
Such a terrible thing
Killing colours
Bleeding red onto black
A living dirge
Its breath to sing
Death in every thing
Grappling with the demon
That would not let you live
Now I read your words
To fathom the shape of darkness
I read your cries
Scrawled over life's face
And you, beauty
Dancing with your demon
In the cold moonlight
Its bite marks
Indelible scars on your heart

I see beauty
Dressed in the veils
Of your anguish
I hear the music
Of your pain
Buried in the notes of
Your dark symphony
Strung like black pearls
Aching against the light.

Port of Messina

1953, For Benito

The Neptunia
Bound for Australia
So far away
Slowly edges out
From the safety
Of the port
Leaving your parents
And the biggest
Part of you
Stranded on land
Your heart beats
From the shore
Clinging to family
Begging you to
Jump ship and swim
Before it's too late
But it's too late already
The Strait of Messina
A fathomless Black
Hole
Unswimmable
By a boy
Torn away
Too soon
From Home
Roots
Blood

KATHLEEN PANETTIERI

The ship heads
Away from you
And all you call
Yourself
Carrying your remnants
With it
Into your future
All you own
Carried in
One small suitcase.

An unknown hero

I.M. Nick Goulas

Modest and humble
His clothes wear his traces
And he no longer there
To choose a shirt, a tie
I will keep this sea-horse
Handle of his clothes brush
Though broken, it holds
A world of memories
Coat-hangers dangle
These remains carrying
The scent of him still
A small corner of
The wardrobe was his
He never measured
Himself by things
Content to swim through
The heroic waters
Of his heritage
The invisible badge
He wore, shone bright
As any medal of honour
He lived like an Ancient Greek
Proud and wise and humble
Unsung, I will sing this song for him
Let heaven ring its bells
Let it be known that I had
An unknown hero for a father.

KATHLEEN PANETTIERI

The cry of the dust

From dust to dreams to dust
I walked today
along this road of sighs
and spent illusions
where the world
is an elephant
on my shoulders
shrouding me
in its grey skin
of disillusion
the past a caged tiger
growling in my veins
its piercing eyes
hunting for retribution
the future a lion's roar
stuck in my throat
the unknown raging
to be known
I walk on the blood
and tears of centuries
stirring up their traces
as I pass
and I heard the dust crying
beneath my feet.

Where wild oats grow

When wild oats come clamouring
on wayward winds,
in voices aching to be familiar,
can you hear their song?
I have heard their song,
an abandoned one,
that needs to belong.

I close my eyes
and feel their secrets
coursing through my veins,
their shadows hidden
in places I have never seen.

There is a past that sleeps
resting in the words
already spoken.
There is a past that weeps
crying in the words
just now awoken.

Where wild oats have
risen their heads
in distant forgotten fields.
Caught by a wind
that yearns to harvest
their soughing murmuring
carrying their sobbing
into an unknowing
and still silent present.

KATHLEEN PANETTIERI

Their curious whispers,
seedlings separated from
long distant roots,
rustling their presence
In my astonished ears,
clamouring for attention.

Burning

I kneel
On hard unforgiving wood
Shrinking into myself
Before the hugeness of an
Imposing altar
Watched by saints with hearts
Bleeding from gilt frames
Hung high
I hear
Hell-fire words
Hurled from a pulpit
Confusion of ceremonial robes
Embroidered with venoms
Of sin and condemnation
I am too small
To bear this weight
Of inherited shame
Squirming in the snake pit
Of my churning stomach
Waves of chants
And heady incense
Stir up a host of questions
That vengeance
Cannot answer
Mystery
Older than I can imagine
Hides in the blue vault
Of a church
Sore-kneed
Head bowed

KATHLEEN PANETTIERI

I parrot pious words
Candles burning down
To molten wax
Smoke drifts upwards
Into the obscurity of
Endless clouds that veil
Heaven's door
I have dipped
My small fingers
Into the font of
Holy Water
But I am not worthy
I am a child
Lying on soft green grass
Beside the shadow of
My bewildered innocence
Feeling estranged from
Sense of self
Staring
At the blue vault
Of the sky
Trying to fathom clouds
Questions buzz
Hot sun burns
Down into my layers.

Like, living

The constant morning
Shatters my sleep
Scattering
And regathering dreams
From the box of secrets
I raided in the night
Spread out in the light
They converge
On the screen
Of my mind
Like, turning fiction
Into fact
Becoming
All the pieces
Of a scattered jigsaw
Whirling
Alive in me
Searching for
Their place
Like, learning the shape
Of forever
Stretching myself
Edging into the fit
Like, being born
Over and over
An endless re-emerging
Into light

Like, slowly remembering
Worlds
Spinning inside
Me
Like, living.
Like, grafting myself
Onto universal skin
Feeling the ache
As it stretches
Assimilating
Its scars
Deep deep within
Like, learning to see
Into an endless mirror
Through the lens
Of the ten thousand eyes.

Bucephalus

Now I lay down these reins
For the battle is over

The kingdom won and lost
Over and over again

To what avail
The kingdom of others

Was never mine to hold
Nor these reins

I relinquish them
What was wild and free

Should be left untamed
We rode into our endless battles

As one body
Or so it seemed

Bucephalus, I set you free
From all shadows

And myself also
Let us ride untamed

Into eternity
Yes, back to the lush green grass of Macedonia

KATHLEEN PANETTIERI

Was that last battle at Hydaspes
Better left un-fought

An heroic fate better
Left un-sought

And when they say our names
They will sound in hollow tones

Across the fields of eternity
That was before I became Alexander

And you my constant stallion
There on the field of dreams

Beyond which all names are one
And each battle already done

So now we have both slipped free
From these bridles of restraint

A boy and horse untamed
Carry me back to eternity

Where we need not weep
For what we thought was lost.

A river of words

Poetry is alive and kicking
And longing to be heard

See how it wears the face
Of this crying world

Its mouth wide open
In a never ending question

Its weeping heart bleeding
Into a river of words

Chanting its hymns and prayers
Celebrating its heights and depths

Sorrow is the deepest word I have heard
Deeper than an ocean of tears

Let me borrow a piece of your heart
To paste upon the walls of my world

I will pour out the words that
Whisper themselves into my soul

They will fly me across an ocean of fears
Unafraid I spread my wings

And open my heart to share
The words it needs to say and

Lend them to the arms of the wind
To carry them where they need to go

Singing of sorrow and hope and
The deep aching mystery of love.

Divergent

How the spy catcher
Is enamoured
Of the spy
How the spider
Hungers for the fly
So I crave that
Which I am not
As though part
Of me was torn away
And abandoned
In the womb
And I expelled un-whole
With this angst
For my antipode
A living burning desire
So that when we meet
In the flesh
We are magnets
Drawn by this sense
A memory of wholeness
Like a broken bridge
Over a yawning gap
That draws me and lingers
Its fingers subtle murmurs
Running through my veins
And clawing at my heart
That dark other of me
Begging me to love it
And bring it home.

KATHLEEN PANETTIERI

This earthenware vessel

Let me soften your shoulders
With a soothing touch
Slacken the grip of rogue tensions
That twist themselves tight
Come let me wash you clean
In gently falling spring rain
So that your soiled beauty
May shine all new again
Let me clear away those
Accumulations of dust
Where the earth has carelessly
Layered itself on your light
And scrape at these tiny
Imperfections that somehow
Become you now like secret
Engravings fired into you lending
An air of exotic allure
Precious little vessel born of clay
Let me place you out here
In the clear light of a new day
So that sun rays can recapture
Your clear and innocent lines
To reflect their joy through you
See how your sturdy tender beauty
Once again so brightly shines
You are old and new and true
Wearing your bounty of history
In an invisible skin of mystery

After the storm

After the storm
Has torn a rage of emotion
from our deepest places
And all the cracks and all the bruises
Are showing up
On our bewildered faces
Is this just a crazy dance of love
We sketch with hesitant feet
Across deserts of unsustainability where
All our differences seem stronger
than our compatibility
Cutting through icy fields of feigned indifference
Our stony glances fly
Like bullets ripping us apart
Moving with our broken rhythms
Two steps forwards, one step back
Until we reach ourselves again
After the storm
Where we danced our dance of pain
Where we stood worlds apart
We come together once again
Torn petals on the stem
You reach out for my hand and recapture my heart
And we are back at the start where
The music of love first captured us.

KATHLEEN PANETTIERI

Fracture

She bent to pick up
The pieces of herself
Stuck them back
On the hanging mirror
And saw a stranger
Reflected there
Now the world
Was spinning backwards
What she thought
Was her life had
Walked out the door
Cancelling out who
She thought she was
Leaving a fractured mosaic
Lying on the floor
She hardly recognised
The reflection she saw
Turned inside out
And upside down.

Like Alice

I cannot breathe
My mother's whisper
Rising like a prayer
Her candle burning up
The claustrophobic air
Of events long gone
Melancholy
Sings its silent song
From the shores of grief
Sadness broods
Stealing like a wicked thief
Into the space
Where memories sleep
And I am crying in the dark
In the rooms of my dreams
Wandering like Alice
Through halls of mirrors
Reflections of long gone faces
My brother staring out at me
My father nodding his wise head
Only in dreams can they
Come to re-visit me
As pages riffle and speed past
The hands of time impatiently
Rushing towards tomorrow's
Endless story writing itself.

KATHLEEN PANETTIERI

The ringing of the bell

1949

The clanging of St Anthony's bell
Sounds on the morning air
Resounding in my head a strange
Dilemma of heaven and hell
Questions thrown as a shroud
Over the day and the future
With no answers that my
Nine year old self can tell
I stare up at the loftiness
Of this house of God

The collar of my school blouse
Is frayed around the edges
It must feel the way I feel
As the stern faced nun
With her cutting tongue
Trims with her scissors
Its unkempt lowliness
It must have been born
With original sin also, falling
Apart right next to my skin
Which I am told bears a stain
Invisible as the silent sound
Of an echoing wail that has
Buried itself deep in my soul
My young self already
Feels tattered frayed and worn
Left fallen and torn outside
Something important that hides
Beyond words that do not jell.

A parting gift

When our mother passed
She left us a gift
That version of herself
We had so deeply missed
Lying there in her hospice bed
So soft and sweet it caught our breath
Cancelling out innumerable hurts
In dark little corners of life
Miracles happen
Floodgates opened, pouring peace
Around that bed
She was our mother, wearing the face
That had only inhabited our dreams
Perfectly smooth and innocent, completely
Stripped of all anguish and anger lines
Death had taken its purgatory with it
The bitterness dissolved
And that other face fallen from her
Like dried out leaves in autumn
Tucking her in for the winter
And laying her to rest
I hope she was born again
In the springtime.

Decidious

See my bare arms reach skywards
Drawing sun rays deep into my core
I am that naked living tree
Everything merges submerges
And re-emerges in me
I wear the shape of the seasons
I move to the rhythms of love
I feel the surge of new growth
I hear the cooing of the dove
The screech of each weary bird
That falls into my open arms
Wooed by the wind song
I move to the rhythm of its dance
I reign in my own deep space
Exposing in unbounded
Explosions of spectral light
That which I am and you are
Robed in buds leaves and flowers
My undying spark ignites the fire
As together we dance up from
My ever burning core to flourish
In orchards of infinite delight
We are deciduous, you and I
The winds of autumn will harvest
Our ephemeral sproutings
Pouring them back into the earth
The world a transient moonbeam
Floating before our eternal eye.

Lanterns

When I stumble through the ashes
of fallen generations,
searching for a compass needle
in the haystack of desolations.
When the road is fraught with indecision
and night falls down like the walls of a prison,
I see a misty light still shining
where love has left its mark
on the hazy windows of my soul.
I stumble warily through the dark
hands outstretched as I ask,
must pain and loss always
be the price of survival?
I shed my thousand skins
and I am back in the cradle,
before the world had opened
my eyes and blinded my sight.
While a song I once heard
in the far far long ago
is running through my mind,
with a nectar that still clings
to my heart's trembling strings.

KATHLEEN PANETTIERI

Toora Loora …baby
Hush now don't you cry
Toora Loora …baby
That old sweet Irish lullaby
for which my heart does yearn.
I see love is waving its lanterns
a little further down the road,
guiding me on my way back home
and longing for my return.

Overture

Crisp early morning
Fresh on my face
I park the car
Move across still
Empty spaces
Pigeons scatter
In disturbed flurries
My passing altering
The direction
Of their moment
Sweeping in a wave
Across their path
They fly off
This way and that
Confused
By my intrusion
Outside the supermarket
A solitary busker
Tunes his violin
Strains of *Beautiful Dreamer*
Weep
Onto the morning air
A legato of single notes
Rising
In a momentum
Of moments

An overture to the day
This ocean of living
Moving waves
In symphony
Each with the other
In a flurry of wings
And limpid notes
I float
Across the car park.

Where wizards play

Don't ask me about perfection
I am a torn creature
Riding on the waves
Of adversity
Where prosperity
Is a dangerous place to be
Inviting envy and thieves
To come stealing
In the night
I ride on waves of colour
Dipped in this melting pot
That has fashioned its world
And strung out on winds
Of changeability
My fate cast on the dice
Rolling down from mountains
With necks stretched to the sky
Ridiculously high to climb
Where possible and impossible
Jostle on the straight lines
Of predictability

KATHLEEN PANETTIERI

Don't ask me about perfection
I am content to play
This game of chance
Living on the spectrum
Of riotous colours
Bleeding into each other
Beyond the rigidity where
Black is wrong and white is right
And colours fade to grey
Let me ride the seesaw
And feel the wind in my hair
And sun and rain on my face
And insecurity pulling me
Like an unseen wizard
On the tides of adventure
Where magic can be smelled
On each current of air
And sprouts like mushrooms
Around the trunk of a tree.

Under a gypsy moon

It must have happened
under a blood red moon
that I was born the child
of a gypsy woman
Not my earth mother but that other
with her face unseen, who bore me
long long ago
It must have happened
in a dream I once had that she
endowed me with her gypsy heart
Pressed into my tiny palm
the silver coin she took from
a stranger's hand and drew
the lines of my fortune there
At nightfall
her eyes are flashing stars
when I become that gypsy child again
wandering in the corridor of dreams
where I have kept this secret
closely tethered to my soul.
One day, I know,
she will come to whisk me away
back to her gypsy place where
her brightly painted caravan waits
at the edge of dreams.
She will coax the aching beauty
of her welcoming song, make it
weep from the strings of her violin
as we ride on a nomad wind
along the streams of the Milky Way

KATHLEEN PANETTIERI

and beyond that wandering
blood red moon
She will shower me again with her
silver coins
falling in torrents like sparkling rain
onto the earth
And I will waken to the sounds
of a new day birthing
Feel her hand pressing my waiting
fortune into my empty palm.

The face of dilemma

It comes welling up from somewhere ancient
Deep inside you
Rage you don't recognise
As yours
You pound at it
Leering from the mirrored face
Before you
You grapple with its intensity
Its smirking face of complicity
You hit it again and again
Want to tear from yourself
This terrifying dilemma
You don't hear the cries for help
The unrecognisable face before you
You want the rage to be gone
From its seething primal place of fear
From the dark stain of colliding memories
You hit it again and again
The victim, the culprit, wearing
The same distorted face
You plead 'not guilty'
A victim wearing a culprit's mask
Manacled, you move
From one cage to another.

Ancestry

The chain of belonging runs backwards
As it runs forwards
I stare into the slowly forming faces of my future selves
And their unknowing of me
In this mutable moment in time
To them I am just a discarded memory
Forgotten and never really known
But they will walk in my discarded shoes
Scuffing my footprints with their own
Mingling their particles of dust with mine
The past and the future mirror themselves in the present
Can they ever understand that I love them?
Or know that our joy and pain are shared
That their images reflect intimate parts of me
My mother lives and breathes in us
My father stirs in his sleep to share in our dreaming
Our unattained dreams may redeem themselves in them
Will they understand those unfinished threads of living
Throbbing in their veins
Belong to the past and future
And somehow I will know myself again in them
That together, knowing and unknowing,
We will continue to trace our ancestry
Backwards and forwards in an
Unending circle of belonging.

A place called home

Now still, now quiet, I breathe
Let thoughts ripple away
Dive into the void that was
Before all the believing began
Before a world had built itself
Into a fortress into a prison

Let go of everything
Step over the edge
Fall into the canyons of unknowing
I wait for the remembering
I wait for the promise
I wait for the cleansing of the flood

Now into the empty chest it flows raw
Pure from the font of emotion wild
And welcoming filling spilling into
The waters of a new baptism
Bringing me home at last and the keys
Placed into my open hand

Now I am my own treasure chest
Full to brimming, spilling onto my
Untethered prodigal tongue into
An impossibility of expression
Words tangling themselves into
Exuberance of joyful arrival, the ark

KATHLEEN PANETTIERI

Brings me to the arms of Alpha and
Omega. Now still, now quiet, I breathe
To complete the circle once again
Tracing and re-tracing myself onto
An infinity of worlds, point to point
Moving into my shadow, into my light.

Out of emptiness

I wear the skin of the world
I feel it holding me tight
I lean upon its bones
And hear its pulse
Within my blood
Don't ask me who I am

I am everyone I see
The best and the worst
Of every you and me
Has the mirror of the world
Borrowed my empty face
To write itself upon.

KATHLEEN PANETTIERI

Shadows and lies

Come out, come out and show your hidden face
Come out from the deep burrows of myself
Where no splinter of light has left its trace
Only pain that hit its coward blow
Pain with its jeering face of bluff
Dressed in the stuff of shadows and lies
Hiding like some monstrous secret
way down deep inside my soul
To ride on the tide of my innocent blood
Convincing me I was no longer whole
Left drowning in your venomous flood

I was born an innocent child
Of the seed of freedom sweet and wild
Come out into the clear light of day
Reveal yourself as vagrant shadow
So I can look you right in the face
And finally just blow you away
Let me unchain my suffering self
From all those broken weary days
Burdened with crooked shadows and cruel lies
Your messages of sorrow and grief
Written in blood by the hand of a thief
And let me gaze into the shining face
Of a blazing innocent new sunrise
All dewy and perfumed like a freshly opened flower
My hands curled once more into fists of power.

Myths of paradise

Both my grandfathers were myths
Spirited away by the Gods of War
To hang amongst their grim trophies
Of the fallen, the missing and the unknown
To their grandchildren, unknown
My mother's father in Northern Ireland a policeman
Scarred by the scapegoat of religion
My father's father in Northern Greece
a family man with a brave heart
Their legacies entwined by the same hands
War and betrayal by their own kind
In Ireland for consorting with the enemy
his Irish catholic wife
In Greece for helping the enemy
Those Italians who turned their backs
Refusing to fight on the side of insanity
Betrayed by the laying down of arms
Betrayed by compassion and love
All, glitches in the machines of war
And the Gods of War did wreak their vengeance

No, I never saw the light in my grandfathers' eyes
Or felt the touch of their hands
Because they were legends who died for love
Their families forced to run like refugees
To find their damaged futures in a distant land
And I, standing in my vantage point of that future
I, the seed they sowed but never
reaped, am here now
Trying to make sense of it all

KATHLEEN PANETTIERI

Sensing the stealth of the traitor's shadow around me
The plunge of the knife in my back
Tracing old threads of pain woven into a magic carpet
Which I have ridden out of their mythological past into
The Aladdin's cave of my life

So we clothe ourselves in our own myths
Anchorage in a fathomless sea of existence
We whisper our reverence to them
Shadows cast upon crumbling walls
As years went hurrying along
Otherworld memories tended in their circles of stones
A refrain of some old haunting song
When all is said and done
Maybe nothing is all that important
We live, we die, everything flashes by
Brief sandstorms flying out towards the limits
Oh, but the centuries overflow with
stories handed down like precious
heirlooms, visited and re-visited
Truth and fantasy mingling like
blood brothers until we in turn
Become our own legends

Dressed in our mortal raiment
Dreaming of immortality, perhaps
We are the myths of paradise
And they whisper about us there
How we wear the flowers
Of the earth in our hair

DOWN A COBBLESTONE LANE   79

How we prance and dance like
children, sequins sparkling
On the garment of the universe
In paradise perhaps they drape themselves
In all those spreading colours
Weeping in a rainbow flood
From the grist of flesh, blood, bones,
When we sailed like Ulysses
Across oceans of imagination
Or flew like wounded birds
Too close to the sun

Do they grant us their homage as we
Fall in and out of endless days
Yearning to be one with them?
Perhaps they dream of us there
Just as we dream of them here
When all is said and done
Maybe everything, each tiny speck, is important
So let me place this flower in your hair
For we, too, are dancing here
Tracing our indelible patterns into
The endlessly falling dreamdust.

KATHLEEN PANETTIERI

Polarities

Every hero needs a villain
Every zero seeks a number
Every enemy is someone's friend
Every beginning has an end
Every up has its down
Even a smile can become a frown
Every tyrant needs a slave
Each coward hides behind the brave
Every big has a small
Every short has a tall
Happy has its sad
Good has its bad
Every girl needs a boy
Every child needs a toy
Every game needs a player
Every dream needs a dreamer
Every war hungers for peace
Every knot needs release
What is false vies
With what is true
Every 'I' needs a ''you'
Be my hero, I will cheer you
When you slay the fiery dragon
Be all these things to me
And I'll be them for you
Let me be your hero
I will rescue you
You can be my saviour
I will confess to you.

The constant garden

I wear the world
Like a cape
Around my shoulders
And it shapes me
With a hold
I can't escape
If I could reach
The other side
Of all that matters
If I could watch
The rise and fall
As the mirror shatters
Watch the pieces
Snatched by the wind
And feel oppression
Lifting from my shoulders
I look at the phone
Waiting mute
Think of you long gone
Scrambled frequencies
Deliver no messages
The distance between
Earth and sky remains
A mutated mystery

KATHLEEN PANETTIERI

Words unformed drip
Like spun silver rain
Into spaces of the heart
Where a constant
Garden keeps on growing
Its roots buried deep
Into unseen places
Beyond the edges
Of the world I wear.

Out of Eden

The straits are narrow
On the way back to Eden
The razor's edge
Set high between rifts
And canyons of duality
I was always guilty
Until proven innocent
Thrown out of Eden
Risen from the slime
Of uncountable crimes
Of all the original sins
Of all the worlds within
Worlds, within worlds
Born of a tainted womb
Wrapped in the skin of shame
Windswept fragments of myself
Counting every breath
Threading itself onto
This tiny borrowed life
Foreshadowed by death
A scavenger for lost innocence
I lean across the schism
Of my shattered and wounded self
I can hear the songbird singing
At the outer edge of dreams
Its lilting song fills my ears

KATHLEEN PANETTIERI

Only in dreams could I be bound
Cast in two separate moulds
My heart lifts and it will carry me
Home, along the misty road to Eden
To gather my wholeness into that
Clear and ever-present moment of naked innocence.

Undone

I remember
When life felt like a ride
On a fast train
I loved to go walking
In the rain
Now I recognise
I am so tired
Of being a prisoner
Of yesterday
It isn't a real place
Anyway
Gone and scattered its pieces
All over my floor
Everything vanished
Things left undone
Collecting dust
I don't want to be there
Anymore

I am opening my door
To the sun
And the day
Those discarded pieces
Didn't fit anyway
I will leave them lying
Where they fell

KATHLEEN PANETTIERI

The wind can
Lift and carry them
Away
Whispering
Unfinished stories
That they tell

I am
Tired of it all
Living with my back
Against the wall
I remember
When life felt like a ride
On a fast train
I loved to go walking
In the rain
I slip back into
The here and now
I hear a whistle blowing
Somewhere again
Rattling down the tracks
And calling me.

Burning pages

Flipping backwards
Through the Book of Days
I am standing again in the late sixties
The weather was fine and
The lakes flowed serenely
Past the entrance
Man had walked on the moon
Printing himself on this page of history

It was mid sixty-nine and our
Little astronauts looked fine
As the weather, in their moon-suits
As they caressed baby kangaroos
And peeped at koalas nestled
In their tall gum tree homes

Calm and serene in repose that day
But a future glimpse, back then,
A riffling of pages forward
Could have seen us engulfed in flames
As red as the moon-suits they wore
That day

There would have been no descent
Into Buchan caves....right place,
Wrong time. Stalactites weeping
Their ice cold tears, holding their
Breath beneath the shuddering
Burning ground.
Can fire and ice ever meet?

KATHLEEN PANETTIERI

Our feet tramping through
The silent caves too far distant,
Then, to sense the waves of doom
Sweeping towards that peaceful
Place. Right place, right time,
For us.

The frightened squeals
Of terrified bush creatures fell silent
On our ears. History's pages
Turned backwards. The future
Burning its way slowly towards us.

The Way

tao

Today I am slathering
The butter on my toast
And enjoying it
Every last bite of it
I am tired of hearing
What is good, what is not
What is going to
Lengthen my life
Or shorten it
I will not skim
The top off life
Today I will not
Practice deprivation
I am tired of worrying
When I will die
How I will die
If I will die
I don't know
How to die
I only know
How to live.

At the intersection

The wheels of the world
Grind slowly and yet more slowly
For there is danger up ahead
The word has spread and spread
From far mountains and deep valleys
Along highways and narrow alleys
Something is coming to meet us
At the intersection of our fear
Do you hear, do you hear?
Will we cover our ears and hide our faces
Leaving the bare bones of our traces
As witness to monumental changes
Wreaking havoc in this year of years.

The grinding wheels of the world
Clank and rattle in deep spaces of our souls
Life will take what we make from
This forsaken and harrowing mess
And we will be shaken to the depths
As we slowly and humbly move
Forward on our fresh oiled tracks
Wheels running smoother and smoother
With our hearts wide open once again
As we strive to weave a better world
For the innocent face of the children
Taken to the brink of the precipice
In this unforgettable year of years.

Inside my box of shadows

There is time enough
To conquer my world,
I will stay close to ground
And smell the earth.
There is time enough
For time is a game,
Now it is now
Then it is then
When is soon enough.
This moment here and this one
Morphing into the shapes
Of years that cast
Their own shadows.
There is time enough
To drown in my own tears
To wear this skin of the victim,
Time enough to face the fears
Hung on the walls of my world.
Inside my box of shadows
I keep the darkness
Locked away
And the pounding feet
Of the past caught
In their own trap.
Here, close to the warm earth
I can smell the indelible print
Of the stain of re-birth.
I will tuck all my pain
Tightly away,
There is time enough
To breathe time away.

KATHLEEN PANETTIERI

Boxed in

Today I am like a slow train
Riding on the monorail of my life
I can't get out of my own way
I weigh myself down with hesitancy
Is there something important
I need to be doing today
The racing wind seems to whisper
But I can only chug along
In low gear as though
I am climbing an invisible mountain
The fountain of youth has flowed
Away leaving just a trickle
Dripping inexorably onto
A worn down stone inscribed
With a story somebody might
Remember hearing over and over
Before in so many better ways
Days strung together like chain mail
Squeezing me in ever tightening armour
Protector and abductor both
Boxing me into repetitive patterns
That shriek for merciful undoing
And a complete release back
Into the stratosphere of my being.

Heartbeat

Three o'clock in the morning and
All is still here on my street
I peer through a darkened window
At the street light blinking at me
As together we patrol the night
Sleepless, my mind awake with questions
I have questioned the earth
I have questioned the sky
Tell me what, tell me who
Tell me all the reasons why
No answers did I hear, not from
The earth, not from the sky, but
I feel the ground firm beneath my feet
I see the sky dark and complete above and it whispers to me
Love is the only answer for
Fear is just another question in disguise
And only I can be the love I know
And my own reason why
That I am, and I am here, witness
To this dark night, this empty street
The sentinel light atop its pole
Petals of the flower, asleep now, share their perfume with me
Stars in the deep velvet sky wink at me.

KATHLEEN PANETTIERI

The night wind whispers to me its question
How many times can a heart break
And still beat to the tune of love?
This self of life, beyond measure,
Knows the tiniest sparrow and
Each grain of sand sifted on passing winds
Each ache, each pang of each troubled heart
It knows itself through me, as I know
Life as myself, with this one heart
That beats to the rhythm of love.

Uriel rising

(archangel of light)

I have sharpened my
Teeth and claws
On the grindstones of grief and grievance
A rude and blustering wind has
worn away
All my too-soft edges
Now I stand eye to eye with life
Comfortable in this skin
Close my ears to words hanging
In spikes of black ice
From the mouth of darkness
I re-clothe myself in the armour of my dignity
The thief who comes to steal from me
Will find chains of gold around my heart
And pillars of steel before my house
And I will not be broken by empty words
Or by hammers and nails that would
hang me up separate from myself
The guardian of souls hovers as I take
each step over the precipice of life
And I can see Uriel rising from
The ghettos of my own distortions
As it rose from the camps of insanity
From the fields of endless battles
From the graves of humanity
As it will always rise
Shattering the black glass of night
Releasing the face of light.

KATHLEEN PANETTIERI

Burning up the night

It's three o'clock in the morning
And I'm lying here awake
There is a dragon in my room
And the night is a burning lake
Wrestling spectres fill my head
And my mind is far too wide
Sandman cast his grains of sleep
Over on the other side
A pale white witch is dancing
With the dragon in my room
Dancing down the clock
To kill the witching hour
I hear their laughter sweeping
Up like hungry flames
Feel their breath of fire in my ear
Grey ash rising on the pale moonlight
Let your fingers take me out of here
Lift me from the cauldron
Of this slow burning night.

Utopia

I have faced
The dragon
I have breathed
Its fire
Felt the pull
Of freedom
The chains
Of desire
I have seen
The temple
Come crumbling down
Stood alone
In my innocence
On shaky ground
I have etched
My dreams
On the aching
Light
Exorcised
My demons
From the breaking
Night

KATHLEEN PANETTIERI

I will return
To Utopia
Barefoot and free
To run through
The green grass
Again
Through the fields
Of home
My days strung
Gentle and free
On daisy chains
And I will lie
Down once more
In the endless
Light.

The lion and the lamb

My mother was a lion
Who chewed on the carcass of life
My father was a lamb
Tied his own hands for the slaughter

I am the daughter
Of the lion's unsated roar
The child of the lamb
Grown into her own wolf

I am the child
Of the moth and the flame
Who burn for each other
Again and again

I am the child
Of the fire and the rain
Who die in each other
Again and again

I am the child
Of pain and its yearning
The dragon's breath, the lion's roar
The seed of peace, the death of ire

I am the child
Of the lion and the lamb
And I will let them lie down together
Here, on the tranquil ground of my being.

KATHLEEN PANETTIERI

Tightrope

I am a firewalker
My burning soul has learned to walk
Upon the hot volcanic stones
Of its own eruptions
I am a levitator
Floating above the dark abyss
Of my own intrigues
I have pulled tricks from the deep
Recesses of my velvet bag
Becoming my own magician and
Waving the wand of my own
Impossible wizardry
Watch me piece together
Sawn-off parts of myself, the woman
Inside my own dark box
Legacy of soul ache, heart break
I am a tightrope walker
Clinging to the razor edge
Of my own polarities
Arms outstretched for balance
Down below, the dark fathomless
Bass notes of my soul music
Up above, the melodic treble
Cosmic notes of my higher self
All around me the metronome of my world.

Resting place

I don't visit the graves any more
They only speak of dust and ash
and impermanency
And if I build a shrine to any one
I build it here within me
It travels wherever I may go
The spirit of their burial place
Custodian of shadows only
That city of the dead
Holds no allure for me
With its symbols planted
Like question marks
I have tasted the grist
Of truth within myself
I remember the things
That stones can never hold
Words of love once spoken
Still come alive in me
The sight the sound the smell of them
The atoms the cells the invisibility of them
I am a monument to all they did
My bones have grown from their bones
Their blood pours through my veins
Their voice still calls in me
If I build a shrine to any one
I build it within my walls
Where does cause end and effect begin?
No, I don't go to the graves any more
No one is buried there.

KATHLEEN PANETTIERI

Yesterday's ghosts

A solitary bird hanging against
A vacant blue sky
The boy on the bike becoming
The man striding to work
Mothers holding the hands
Of tomorrow's urgencies
The rising sun will slowly burn the day away
The moon's blank face turned the other way
The black cat meows, stares at me
With huge demanding eyes
Dog walkers pass with their leads and commands
You come to stand beside me
Our reflections caught
In the window's transparency
As we sip our coffees,
Think our transient thoughts,
Stare at the day,
Listen to passing sounds, mechanical,
So mundane, so mysterious
Endless streams of details
Running to keep up with the day
Building into brooding pyramids
Of anticipations, disappointments
How soon the moon will turn its face
How quickly the night will swallow
And set in stone everything
Yesterday's ghosts staring back
Sphinx-like as together we go
Whirling around in space
Falling in and out of days.

The appointed time

The wine is red
With a perfume that
Soothes my head
We have pushed
The night long
Past midnight
The wine the bread
The perfect time
Is this the time
The stars have saved
For dreamers?
Tomorrow is a shadow
Begging at the door
What have we to give
But undigested yesterdays
Abandoned on the floor
The time has come
The piper is calling
The candle burns down
Waxen stream falling
Raise a glass
To the hours hanging
By a thread
Entwined our hands
Break the bread
Our thirsty lips
Taste the wine.

Undercover lover

Have you been out there chasing dreams again
Scraping your wings against sharp edges
Now you're back here on the floor again
Undercover of the moon
Staring out your window as shadows gather
In the darkness of your room

Is the moon your one true friend tonight
Casting silver light into your gloom
Watching as you climb into your lonely bed
Desire still pumping in your veins
Hope still drumming in your head
Could your lover be that shadow man waiting out on the moon?

Watching over you as you sleep
Soft beams resting gently on your cheek
Is love simply waiting between the pages as you write
The dreams that fill the emptiness of every lonely night
Your undercover lover bringing in the dawning light.

Walking on water

We've been struggling in the water
Trying to rise above its depths
Like lambs before the slaughter
Crying with our failing breaths
If I could walk on water
I would part the waves for us
So we could move through shallows
Towards that haloed moon
If I could breathe on water
And turn it into wine
Would troubles burst like bubbles
Up above the water line
Should we cast our bread out
Upon these ancient waters
And you take my hand to hold
Will it come back multiplied tenfold?
If I could be that miracle
We both still hunger for
Speak with tongues like an oracle
Would we grieve and weep no more
If I could walk on water
I would turn the tides around
And we could walk together
Towards that promised land
Kneel with me before this altar
Carved from ancient stone
I have heard it whisper to me
When I am all alone.

Caprice

There is a feisty breeze
Puffing out its breath today
Why do I tremble
On this cusp of change
Like a dewdrop clinging
To the edge of a leaf
Am I just a moment in time
Or is time just a moment in me
Feeling that breeze stirring
The tree where I have landed
On my way to the unknown
To which somewhere
Will I be thrown?
Or in which direction
Will some capricious
Movement take me
Whirling me into its dance?
Am I just a whim on
Some fleeting breath
Of a strange enormousness
Engulfing and enfolding me
Moving to its own rules
That make no sense to me.

Finite

I'm sorry
We were not vast as
The endless sky above
I'm sorry
If by being me
I have caused you pain
I'm sorry
If I was
Not perfect once again
I'm sorry
I was not
Better smarter stronger
I'm sorry
We are not
Together any longer
I'm sorry
I wasn't worthy
Of your endless love.

KATHLEEN PANETTIERI

Strange bedfellows

I live on the edge
Of a cry of pain
And a cry of joy
The sibilant sounds of
My father's soft sensitivity
The harrowing howl of
My mother's wailing banshee
These strange bedfellows
Sleeping inside of me
My inheritance
To be born or to die
In a scream of pain
Or a joyous cry
Every birth every death
A kind of homecoming
So why am I afraid
Of this abyss inside of me
I tread water in the shallows of me
Across the surface of this living lake
Whose magnitude I cannot glean
This enigma brooding unseen
Yet I can feel the depths of me
Anchored to infinity
Like an ache like a promise.

Resurrection

and they came to the tomb
and found it empty

A tirade of tangling tongues
Busy slicing their way down
Through buried parables
That once fell on our deaf ears
A pounding of running feet
The frantic past racing
To catch up with our present
Now it's a helter-skelter
Of words tripping over themselves
As the parcels all so neatly tied
And buried in their little tombs
Are irrevocably ripped apart
I miss you from the days
When we knew just what to say
Our words pure and clear as bells
I miss you now our desperate
Stories have gotten in the way
How could we not know how
Love can dance with controversy
How truth can embitter tongues
Our present just the tainted gift
Of an inevitably unravelling past

KATHLEEN PANETTIERI

Hope hangs trembling up there
High on the Southern Cross
As our busy fingers unwrap
Our tight empty little resentments
Are we lost from each other
Or heading towards a resurrection?
Can we rise to forgive ourselves?

Wood smoke signals

the night air
has that autumnal
wood smoke
in the air smell
intimations
of winter
open fire
on the hearth
toasted marshmallows
on forks burning
our fingers
hot chocolate
flushing our cheeks
huddled together
listening to
ghost stories
deliciously scary
our faces eerie
in dying firelight
seeing shapes
forming and breaking
in glowing sparking
crackling logs
falling asleep
being carried to bed
tucked in tight
eyes squeezed shut
against scary shapes
dancing on walls

KATHLEEN PANETTIERI

I sniff this
smoky night air
crawling with
simmering
shimmering
signals sent
from the past
rippling into
goosebumps
on my skin.

Mirror eyes

You fell down the rabbit hole
Into a confusion of warrens
Hiding the terror of secrets and lies
Swathed in sombre cloaks of pain
I feel your mournful sobbing
Throbbing deep in my veins
You invite me into your sadness
Into the maelstrom of your fears
Your tears running like rivers
Over the threshold of my soul
We are one in a world of questions
Seeking answers from each other

Through deep weaving warrens
Hung with dark distortions
Perplexity mirrors itself on angles
Of your quicksilver face
I hear your lost cry echoing
A forlorn weeping lament
Look away from dark rivers
Seeping in to submerge your soul
Away from cheating mirror eyes
That only want to tell you lies
Unwrap those cloaks of pain
That hide your immaculate face.

KATHLEEN PANETTIERI

Disturbed

Old wounds
Festering beneath time's wrinkles
Accumulations of scar tissue
Tracing the trajectory of pain
They linger inside us, disturbed
They, too, cry as we do
Yearning for a merciful release
A settling of the ledger of life
A restoration of ideal symmetry
Complete erasure of ugly scars
Equilibrium of our bruised hearts
The closure of a perfect healing.

A la carte

The ambience
Feels just right
Lighting subdued
But not too much
Low buzz of conversation
Gentle clatter of cutlery
This ritual of dining out
People at their little
Separate tables
So modern
So ancient
Raw edges of
The primitive
Neatly trimmed away
No hunting here
Beyond scrutiny
Of the A la Carte
Menu of choice
No tearing apart
Of bloody carcass
Or scrambling for
The lion's share
Fine dining
Good food
Soft firelight
Maybe a candle
Burning, flickering
In a stranger's eyes

KATHLEEN PANETTIERI

The deference of the service
Gathered here around
Ancient flames
Of a modern gas log fire
Glasses clink
In celebration
We can forget
The beast still rises
Where choice is lean
Outside our civilised patch.

The virtuoso

I hear your sadness
In tones of a slow falling rain
On a day turned to grey
I, too, have felt this way
Have heard these crying notes
Caught by passing winds in
An adagio of aching loss
Running through my veins
I hear you say "I miss him"
Your voice heavily playing
A deep andante of disappointment
The spirit moving in us, the virtuoso
Playing us like instruments
Memories, the bow sliding in tempo
Across the pliant strings of our
Bleeding and yielding hearts
Drawing from us the cadences
Of our pain, our losses, our grief
Then building in loving rhythms
The crescendos of our joy.

Makeshift Living

The homeless have moved
To Chelsea by the Bay
They have heard that
It is a swell place to stay
They sleep with their reflections
Beside empty shop fronts
Mattress and blankets spread
On cold pavements, their
Bits of clutter arranged
In their decor of the times
People walk past and say
What is happening to
Chelsea by the Bay
The homeless shuffle through
The day knowing words
Will get them nowhere
And nowhere is where
They will sleep tonight
On a makeshift bed
Beside their reflections hung
In another empty shop window.

Two Step

Trees dripping
Last night's rain
That stain
On the carpet
Telling last night's tale
Unmade beds
Heads askew
Light bruising
Bloodshot eyes
Last night's pain
Stepping out with
Today's blank face
One step forward
Two steps back
Smudging the lines
From night to day
Messy pages
Stained with life.

On Chelsea sidewalk

She is singing on the sidewalk
As people pass her by
A little shabby and a whole lot worn
There are days she wishes
She had never been born
Her lyrics falter on a sigh
While she strums her melancholy
Counts her meagre pile of coins
Hides the tears she wants to cry
She is waiting for the miracle
To come and show its face
Waiting for the miracle
To be her saving grace
Close your eyes and make a wish
Drop a coin in her guitar case
She could be me, she could be you
This could have been your choice
Broken dreams on Chelsea sidewalk
Hiding in the refuge of your voice
Why would you pass her by
As she sings on the sidewalk
Waiting for the miracle
To come and show its face.

Unmasked

If you walk with the devil he will
give no quarter

Lead you like a lamb to your own
slaughter

Fete you like a movie star, invite you
to his pleasure dome

If you walk with the devil you will
learn to hiss and scream

Your dreams will turn to ash, that
vision of heaven

Will wither and crash you on
the brink of hell's walls

Here no wings flutter, no bells ring
to whom can you yell your pain

When the wind whips the screams
right out of your mouth

Drops them into that pit of fire. Here
is where you cannot stay

Here is where you learn how to pray
there is only one road back

From hell. You make up your mind
no need for signposts now

Just follow your own footprints
and those crumbs of contrition

You dropped along the way and get
the hell out of there

Refined in your own furnace
of affliction, you can kiss

The devil goodbye and leave him
to his own machinations

He was never more than a giant
shadow burning itself up

On those walls. His face was sweet,
you thought you knew his name

But he was always a walk on your
own dark side. Unmasked, you take

That road out of inferno to all
you left on the other side

DOWN A COBBLESTONE LANE

This thing called love

For the love of
someone,
for she had been told
of love,
she disrobed
and fell down
upon the altar
of her own yearning.
She peeled away
her layers,
one by one
skin bone
flesh blood,
to reach the regions
of her heart.
For the love of someone
she tore herself
apart,
until she lay
in broken pieces
around the shadow
of her self.
Through a blur
of bitter delusion
she gazed upon
her shattered self,
her heart broken
and used
her body battered
and abused.

KATHLEEN PANETTIERI

Then for the love
of her wounded
and weeping self
she stretched out,
into her own
wilderness,
to gently gather
one by one
each broken piece
and patch them
together again.
She robed herself
in sunshine,
taking herself
by the hand,
she walked into
the meadows of dawn
her search for love
now over;
and lay down upon
its altar
of meadowsweet
and clover.

Hurts

Hurts are the little creatures
She tends to in the dark rooms
Of herself.
She, their captive
She, their keeper, their flame
They rear their heads in X-rated
Flashbacks from the movie of her life
Follow her out into the world, hiding
Behind the sullen screen of her eyes
Bandaging herself around them
Hating them but needing their
Junkie-fix powering her through
The quagmire of living. Feeling and
Seeing each throbbing reminder
Of their affliction. Gashes
That cut her down to size. Bruises
That kicked her into submission
Welts measuring her worth. Words
That won't unspeak themselves
Stoking the fire that makes her burn
The fiery red spikes of her hair scream
Their warning not to get too close
Her black painted fingernails curved ready
Down in the ashy dungeon of her bolthole
Wounded, cowering within her small animal self
Trust has become the enemy.

Jericho falling

When you are sleeping
On a bench in the mall
With everything you own
Stuffed into one bag
You know you're in a nose dive
And headed for a fall
On a collision course
With yourself
But you're just so darned
Tired, you don't give a damn
You just need to sleep and get
away from it all
Exposed, you close your eyes
Your Jericho walls have fallen
The last trumpet call has sounded
You fall asleep hoping that there
Really are angels and a heaven
It's cold without walls
Friends have deserted like rats
You've given up on the
Whole darned thing
You wish the world away
As curious strangers look and pass you by
And your name is just another
Whisper on the wind.

Law of attraction

Our eyes locked across
A crowded room
We were magnets
North and south
My negative
Poleaxed
By your positive charm
You buzzed
Like a swarm of bees
In my breast
Drawn closer, closer
Until I fell
Into your nest
I have climbed
My Everest
To be by your side
To be caught in
Your avalanche of lies
Down, down, down
De-magnetised
Back on solid ground
Deciphering a dream
Was there a grain of truth
Buried there?
Learning the mathematics
Of the rule of attraction
One plus one equals two
Two minus one equals
Alone

KATHLEEN PANETTIERI

I rub my bruises
Remove your stings
From my burning flesh
Your stain from
My empty hands.

As dead trees fall

Sketch me onto the walls of history
This shared story of our humanity
Bury me deep into its mystery
I have felt soft rain fall upon my face
Listened to the storm drumming in my ears
I have breathed deeply the sharp scent of pines
Leaning skywards on the slopes of Etna
Heard the rumbling bass voice of Stromboli
Spewing its fire-works on the dark night sky
I have known thunder pounding in my breast
Stood alone on the crest of unknowing
I have felt black stones dropping one by one
Onto the barren floor of my lost soul
I have hung this string of pearls on my neck
Dripping their salty tears onto the earth
Dragged all my fears into life's raging fire
And felt the heat of desire burn in me
I have heard the beating wings of the dove
My heart has ridden on the flame of love

Let me now sit calmly by my hearth side
Content to reflect on each passing dream
Knowing I am a part of everything
Though broken and battered I may have been
The sun also rises for me each day
This endless tide has borne me on its waves
Now, deeper and deeper and deeper still

The umbilical cord of life draws me
Towards the unseen cavern of its womb
I have said goodbye to so many things
These last few attachments, though
strong, will be
Wrenched from me when that
moment is decreed
My roots torn from the ground
as dead trees fall
Having bled their sap to feed the hunger
So I, too, will take the shape of re-birth
Wrap me in a blanket of memories
And hold me ever closer to your heart
For I will be those new eyes witnessing
This glorious, this inglorious dream.

Mother and child

Sometimes it can take a lifetime
To learn to be a mother
To learn to be a mother's child
Entwined from conception
Until at that instant of birth
Mother and child stare into
Strange and challenging worlds
Mothers and daughters
Mothers and sons

Down paths of constant change
Over patterns already drawn
In the unsettled dust of the past
We rise to challenge each other
Struggle to define our roles and
Sometimes tear at each other
Unknowingly pull each other down
Born onto the same enduring stem
We are its roses and its thorns

Spreading out over a life's journey
We never can know just how
Things will gradually unfold
Or what is the real story being told
At times seemingly too far apart
And then suddenly heart to heart
Deeply impacting each other's lives
In moments that truly define
This delicate enduring relationship

KATHLEEN PANETTIERI

Then comes an irreversible moment
When we stand looking back
By walking through the fire
Being burnished by its heat
We see through each other's eyes
We have learned to understand
How each flame holds the depth
And the breadth of endless love
We have learned what it takes to
Be mothers, daughters and sons.

Mercy

The evening news is full of woe
We're drowning here and

There's nowhere to go
It's India now that has been cursed

In this descent into hell
Have we yet reached the worst

Have mercy on the beggars
Stranded on the streets

Eyes dimmed of the light
Mercy for the street-walkers

With emptied eyes
Rendered unto the night

Mercy for the children
Born into our bitter chagrins

Mercy for our endless stories
Branded in tongues of fire

Upon our burdened souls
Lost and searching for direction

A leap over the edge
A collision with our Achilles' heel

Swinging between chasms
Of our own extremes

Stumbling like fallen angels
With torn and useless wings

The hooded marauder brings
Words of our broken prayer

To hang like despair in the air
Where only the wind's voice sings

Must we beg for hope
For the hopeless

Must we beg for innocence
For the tainted ones

Must we beg for mercy
For our vagabond souls

We dream of the heavens
That we rendered unto hells

We remember a song once heard
Receding into the distance

In a plaintive tolling of bells
We stare at the sky and wait

Like beggars in a land of plenty
We wait for mercy to fall on us

The trial of error

Amongst a great rattling of stones
The tomb of an unsettled past is excavating itself
Spewing up the face of Error and
Binding it to the lashing post of Conviction

The messenger birds have risen
Released to fly finally home to roost
With their cryptic scripts of the
Unforgiven and the unforgotten

Placing their garbled accusations
In the hands of all the Innocents
Summoned as prosecutors and witnesses
Bearing their scales of justice
Their empty urns

Ready to capture Mercy's gentle rain
Their whispers fall on Error's ears
You were simply a miscalculation
To be erased from the granite face
Of Truth

Challenging one by one and
Quashing all protestations from
And all charges brought
Against the slowly disintegrating face
Hanging accused before a jury of its peers

KATHLEEN PANETTIERI

Armed with their unearthed stones
Of self-righteous intent
Which one will wear the Cheshire grin
Hurl the first stone then disappear
In a flurry of pigeons' wings.

Between the beats

Measure for measure
The throbbing music of the world
Never stops but rests
Between the beats it pulls
Me into deep silence

Today, the air is clear
The wind wraps the promise
Of eternity around me
Infinity reigns in realms
Of its own deep silence

Deep silence
Waiting like a conductor
For my music to awaken
And lend itself freely
To every heady beat.

The Land of True

Where have all those moments of certainty gone
When I thought I knew that I could comfort you
I remember when stars were in your eyes
How they would hide behind tears that you cried
When you flew far away on your magic carpet ride
Were you chasing the stars that escaped from your eyes
Or the thieves who would steal your shimmering buried treasure
Rubbing your lamp and counting wishes like Aladdin
Fickle wishes that wouldn't come through, searching for
That magic Land of True that was always there inside of you
Though that misty veil of all the world's fallen tears
Had hidden it away far beyond your view
And when your heart was aching and you could feel it breaking
Could you feel my heart beating right there by your side
Now you are crying all those grown up tears
And I can no longer wipe them away or
Pull down the stars that hang in the skies
To place back in your hurting and crying eyes.

Language of the night

Listening to the sounds
Of my own breathing
Counting
The beats of my own heart
I am a part of all of it, says
The whispering voice of the dark
Hearing
The lone call of a night bird
Remembering
The first one I ever heard
Stillness and movement
These waves I sail upon
And we are here ready
In our tall dream ships
Heading into the estuary
Of eternity again
Me and you, my friend
Again, once again
Listen to the sounds of the earth
The pulsing and the groaning and
The stretching of new birth
Was that your voice I heard
In the silence of the night?
Was that your lantern I saw
Trembling there in the dark?
Was that your hand in the mist
Reaching out as you sailed past?

Was there something that I missed
In the deep deep silence of the dark?
The sounds of my own breathing
The beating of my own heart
That melancholy fleeting tone
Comes to find me when I'm all alone
A wordless voice that speaks to me
In its own language of the night.

Wounded bird

Somebody has to love
the wounded bird
Rescue it as it writhes
upon the ground
Hold it and feel
its shudderings
of pain
Hear its screeching
mournful sound
Gather and hold it
gently in the hand
Until it heals
and learns to trust
The immensity of sky
once again

KATHLEEN PANETTIERI

One morning in Eden

This morning my eyes are mesmerised by
Golden arrows of sunlight streaking
Through the kitchen window
Dancing around my bowl of apples
Polishing bright green, bright red
I am pierced by the arrow
Of undeniable desire, I pick up
An apple and take a bite
This is how it starts, just one tiny bite
The apple comes willingly to share
In this feast
Teeth sinking in, crunching, juices
Flowing, each to each, savouring,
One irresistible bite after another
Consuming right down to the core
The apple discarding its seed, letting
It fall back down to feed the dust
Consuming and renewing
This is how we live This is how we die
This is how it started
One morning in Eden.

Casualty of war

He said,
She said,
In escalating voices
Setting the earth to tremor.
Until windows shatter
And walls fall
And something unfixable
Finally dies.
Nothing left to do
But bury the illusion,
Let it sink into
The surreal with
All the dead things.
What was real was
The first thing to go.
Unseen, unrecognised,
Love was always the first
Casualty of war.
And still the one thing
That can survive.

KATHLEEN PANETTIERI

The silent deep

You have woken feeling cold
and the temperature has dropped.
You know you are getting old
but your beating heart hasn't stopped,
it punctuates the sound of dark.
These edges of the night are stark.
You reach out to the mystery
you know you are travelling blind,
stepping off your page of history
who knows what you will find.
You are hoping for eternal light
but there might be only endless night.
Now I lay me down to sleep
I pray the mystery, my soul will keep.
The night belies the certainty of day,
You twist, you turn, this way, that way.
In the wee small hours when you can't sleep
The unknown looms, the silent deep.
Visions of infinity, just beyond sight,
Whispers of immortality, mute in the night.

Crucifixion

See the blood red roses
unsheathe their shiny thorns
weaving their circlet
of doom to crown
the head of innocence.
Felled by the axe of attrition
a tree stands lifeless
a gift for innocent hands
to drag its load of guilt
through the jeering crowd,
to hang it against a blackened
and star-crossed sky.
The milky breath of innocence
falling to the dust then rising
and rising again and again
its tiny sweet face embedded
in its cradle of petals.
Thorns sharp and threatening fall
all around the waiting trees
their stakes rooted deep deep
in the heart of the ground.
The tremors of distant thunder
hurled from the clouds
have penetrated the earth
echoing in the raucous voices
of doom heard all around.
Where the cross has left its mark
on the centuries weeping at its feet
the hooded mask of guilt
still rises to suffocate and
crucify the face of innocence.

Night bird

I heard a night bird calling
Its throat piercing the deep silence
Note by note dripping golden motes
Into the dark well of night

I heard its last song rising
Plaintive like a prayer
Wings gliding velvet smooth
Reverent on the hushed night air.

Spirit of place

Cry, the burnt country
Now, even the desert weeps dry tears
While hope lies shrouded in slumbers
Under the burning embers

Trees have been felled by angry fire
The spirit of homes
Chokes on windblown ash
Pride of place devoured

In the clash of turncoat winds
And greedy red flames
Snapping and snarling
Like litigant politicians

Vying for supremacy
Wind and fire dying as they
Grapple in each other's arms
Blighted landscape now a cemetery

Spirit of water, Spirit of light
Spirit of earth and sky
Swallow the bloodied bones of contention
Follow your flurried heart's pure intention

KATHLEEN PANETTIERI

The road runs in a swirl of dust
Down to the riverside
Caught and carried by the light
The river flows thirstily towards
Its encounter with the sea

Where tides tangle then tear apart
An exhausted wind catches the waves
And rides them as they endlessly
Crash towards the shore

Spirit of all things, you belong in all place
The wind carries your secret voices
On the wings of the burning day
And hidden in the dark cloak of night

Spirit of water, Spirit of light
Spirit of earth and sky
And they will come by road, by river, by sea
To find you wherever you may be.

Wind song

The day
Grows weary
We sit here in its
Limp stillness
Nothing moves
Nothing speaks
Shadows wait out on the
Edges of the waning light
For evening to call
Them home
A soft zephyr wind
Stirs then rises
Fans the dying
Face of day
With invisible fingers
Teases the inertness of
Hanging wind chimes
With its secret whispers
The silent wind lifts
Finds its voice
Singing its song to us
In tuneful cadence
Of lilting notes
As it rises further
Dancing with the jangling
Crescendo of the chimes
Their duet a secret language
Of caressing harmonics
And wind kisses

　　　　　　　　　　KATHLEEN PANETTIERI

The setting sun and rising moon
Spill their magic into
The mysterious spaces
Between sounds
The silent wind
The talking chimes
Descending dark
All cast their spell
And suddenly
The day
Disappears.

Easy like a warm spring day

Comfortable, like my favourite chair
Always happy to see you standing there

Welcome, as the first light of dawn
After a long and sleepless night

Your smile, wide like a safe harbour
Your hand, soft upon my shoulder

Easy, like a warm spring day
No need to worry about what to say

Let words flow in their own natural way
To come and go and leave no stain

Like the spread of a rainbow after rain
Across an open cloudless sky

Lucky, to have your friendly face
Walk right in to share my space

No subterfuge or hidden games
No pointing fingers asking why

Your company, such an easy place
To share a welcome cup of solace

You sitting here with me
Allowing me to be myself.

Never enough

Go away sun, leave me with melancholy today
She steals into my room knowing how I feel
Colours have run out of the world anyway
We stand here etched in shades of black and grey
Is this ice that runs coldly in my veins?
Our worn out words have emptied themselves
Of anything worthwhile left to say
Falling like daggers on that world we tried to share
Ripping our pretty coloured canvas into useless shreds
I have stood at this doorway of loss before
I swore I would never pass this way again
But the world is such a greedy lover
It draws you in and in to its web of allure
Then buries its pain deep inside of you
And you with your hope trailing its petty slogan
Pleading to the sky, pick me, pick me
Let me be the one to wear that happy face
You were never enough for such a fickle place.

Clouds and rainbows

There are days like this
When even my make-up
Can't hide me from myself
So, I don't bother with subterfuge
I go naked into the day
The map of my face on display
Tracing my defects onto the day's mirror

Until the evening bells start tolling
Telling me another day is over
And I can lay me down to sleep it off
The cycles, the symbols,
Stumble into my dreams
The numbers that hide behind other numbers
Patterns forming and re-forming

Lives that blink and come and go
A stream of stars connecting it all
And should I fall and someone find
Me at the confluence of days
We will sit and discuss the reason
For numbers or patterns
To which we are both integral

Sounding out the resonance of it all
In an endless stream of words
I will paint on my bravado
Dress myself in clouds and rainbows
Go swirling around as part of it all.

Family portrait

One moment in time
When we stepped out of ourselves
And got lost
In the eye of a camera
All polished up in our Sunday best
Wearing our special smiles
Everyday costumes left in a
Disgruntled heap
Outside the door
Snap ...click ... the ... camera ...
Invents its own still life
Version of us
We hurry to gather up
Our own little fictions and
Step back into character.

A sensible choice

"Such a sensible choice"
enthused the elderly sales
assistant as I turned
to catch my reflection
in the mirror. Shrouded
in drab, sensible grey
I caught a glimpse of a
narrow, uninteresting future.
Years of wear, she promised,
my tender young life quickly diminishing
into a handful of sensible coats.
"At least ten years, my dear
you'll get lots of wear",
She was so convincing.
My first solo shopping trip
weighed heavily on my mind
as I rode the train back home,
conjured ways to enhance
that dependable grey with
colourful scarves and brooches.
My mother was aghast
"There's no way you're
wearing that coat", muttering
darkly about the elderly assistant
and my tender sixteen years.

KATHLEEN PANETTIERI

Next day, back on the train
and into the city, my mother
determined to do battle.
"All that money, so terribly
unsuitable", she marched
me back into the store.
Mortified, the coat was duly
returned and we sorted through
the coat racks. Triumphantly
my mother presented me
with an armful of dazzling colour.
Delightfully frivolous and
brightly irresistible, a new coat
in startling rusty-orange wool
with huge shiny black buttons.

Entirely unsensible and warm
as toast, I was a sight for sore eyes
as I stepped onto life's roller coaster
wearing my bright rusty-orange coat.
And still to this day, my eyes
will always choose colour
over drab and sensible grey.

Now rider

for Uly
biking through Vietnam

You feel the grip
Of the handle bars
Nestled in your palms
The road stretching out
Like an invitation
A roar of energy
Under you
As you rev the engine
Up ahead the mountain calls
Down below sea glistens
You start to move
Wind fingers your skin
Joy rumbles up
From deep inside
Moving faster now
Smells of adventure
Tease your nostrils
The shape of your destiny
Etches itself onto each curve
Of the glistening bitumen
Leading down from the mountain
A cagey freedom
Hops on for the ride
Your life calls
You start eating up the road
You drop a load of care
Head towards the mountain.

KATHLEEN PANETTIERI

On dragon-fly wings

Lately, while walking along a well-worn pathway
Through a park where children play,
A dragon-fly drew close to fly along with me
Fluttering its gossamer wings
As it seemed to count my steps.
The sun shone freely down on me,
A soft breeze teased my hair
Whispering its secrets to the trees
While all of nature played in tune
Let me drift away on a day like this
On soft cotton-wool clouds,
Fly away on dragon-fly wings
Let me hear the first bird that sings.
Let me see with the eyes of the oracle
Let me be the face of the miracle.
I want to feel what a mountain feels
When its peak has reached the sky,
Spread my arms to touch the inner
And outer edges of every single thing.
Then let me fall back down to earth
As the seed of a brand new birth.
I was born in the year of the dragon
Child of the fugitives of war
Born to black-outs and lean times
Scarred with the seal of strife.
Let me see again with newborn eyes
The blaze of the first sunrise,
Feel the first fluttering of ancient wings
As I walk my first faltering steps and
Hear the song of the very first bird that sings.

Winter haiku

Listen to the rain
Drumming on the window pane
Its haunting refrain

Wintry days are here
Pelting rain and huge hail stones
All the parks are bare

Angry, howling winds
Thundering rain on tin roofs
Gutters overflow

Water-coloured streets
Umbrellas like parachutes
Move in slow motion

Falling knives of rain
Wind plays havoc with your hair
Puddles everywhere

Mist on the hill top
Probing fingers of sunlight
Tease the mist away

Morning on the Bay
Swelling waves salute the day
Ferry's on its way

KATHLEEN PANETTIERI

Jack Frost comes to stay
Icy fingers on your skin
Woollen caps and gloves

Another cold snap
Pale, watery, winter sun
Boots and overcoats

Snail-paced cars and trams
Honking horns and tempers flare
City traffic jam

Winter traffic snarl
Screeching brakes, slippery streets
Frantic wiper blades

Winter has ordained
Yet another foggy day
Sing your blues away

Rain, rain go away
Come again another day
Somewhere far away

Lament of the unreturned soldier

Gallipoli

I saw your face
On the battleground
Of desolate dreams
We both were there
In that cold dank place
Of deathly schemes
We both lie dead
Our blood spreading red
Into the cold cold ground
I saw the gunfire blast
Heard the cannons roar
When the sky fell down
They laid us under the cross
With our broken dreams
Deep in this foreign soil
When we were boys
With our wooden toys
We played war games
Our flags of peace
Flying alongside
Our flags of war

KATHLEEN PANETTIERI

Two soldier boys
Toy guns of war
Where we kept score
Now the toys are gone
The guns are real
And I can hardly feel
Brother, my brother
Our blood is red
Brother, my brother
Please don't play dead

Movement in two parts

(i)

Silver strands of moonlight
Filtering through the trees,
Shifting hands of midnight
Stir up buried memories.
Sounds of the night calling
Sands of time keep falling.
Legato of lost and found
Leaves fluttering to the ground.
A concert of perfect sound
Connecting threads, vibrating chords.
Rich harmonies of dark and light
Spaces between black and white.
Motes of dust and tinkling notes,
Dancing across this keyboard
Meeting across this spectrum,
Of one perfect seamless music.

KATHLEEN PANETTIERI

(ii)

When the darkness comes,
You can hear the lost note cry
A staccato beat into the skies,
Hello to the phantoms of the night.
A distant echo, its rich legato
Of lost and found, high and low.
This perfect pitch holds its breath
Then rises up towards the light.
Point and counter-point
The music of the ages.
The agony, the ecstasy,
Its own pure tenor of harmony.
A symphony that rages,
Hello to the aching light
The music of the breaking light,
Its movement in two parts.

Café blues

We are in lockdown
So I must imagine myself
Sitting in a small café
In one of Melbourne's
Bustling groovy lanes
Watching the world go by
Ordering a café latte
I sip with a comfortable sigh
Pondering on the benefits
Of raisin toast versus
Scrumptious avocado smash
So easy to replicate
You might say
In your own sparkling kitchen
But no, it's not the same
I realise as it slips
Out of questioning reach
It's an experience I crave
The delicious smells, the voices
Chattering and tangling
My senses with enjoyment
There in that vibrant environment
I am one with the bustling
Teeming atmosphere, imagining
I could be anywhere in the world
But I am just dreaming
While Melbourne is sleeping.

KATHLEEN PANETTIERI

Tear down your walls

Hey there, woman
with your high heel stride
and your red coat swagger
Your eyes drawn to your red rag reflection
in the distraction of every
passing shop front window
Heels clatter clatter on concrete
pavements
the city burns with the red fire
of a million dreamers
Tell me how it feels living
within your skin
surrounded by those million layers
Your bright artificial smile and
painted face
hide the child within
trapped in an eclipsing moment
when the dark came down
Deep down beneath
your red coat swagger
live the bruises the scars the wounds
Can you strip them from the hide of you
to rescue that innocent crouched and waiting
Where dreams have burned to ash
her voice is barely a whisper
calling to you across the hungry years
To take that elliptical turn inwards
To tear down your walls and set her free
Then tell me how it feels living in the real you.

Mea Culpa

Should I wander with my young self through the hall of mirrors
Visions of long gone days, reflections half-forgotten
Don't abandon me to this place where
images do confound
Or leave me stumbling in this forest
where shadows lie all around
I have come upon a crystal pool that
mirrors the upside down forest
Twisted branches of distorted
trees hang weirdly in its depths
Should I gaze like Narcissus into this
bottomless pool
Of dead guilty faces floating with blank eyes lifeless
They dream no more, stark and stiff
like the tangled forest trees.
Don't make me stare like the fabled
Evil Queen
Into the pool of my own mirror, for I
fear the enemy lurking there.
I may be the face
of my own cruel delusions
The clown tumbling around in my own circus.
Should I dive into this forgiving pool
whispering to me of perfection,
Will I rise to the surface pure as
Snow White
No longer to hang on this cross with
the apple stuck in my throat.

Can you, my young self, erase your
own distortions and loosen
These chains you placed, unwittingly,
around my world.
Because you were there and I was still
to come
I cannot go alone.
Dare we dive, together, into that crystal pool?

Universal child

Who are you, beneath
Celtic/Greek blood moving in you

beneath crazy Irish abandon
tapping and stamping its feet

cutting air into defiant shapes
tracing brave patterns on the earth

arms that would be wings held
rigid at your side. Who are you,

beneath sombre importances
of philosophers and the strumming

bouzouki measuring intricacies
of clicking fingers, pounding feet

Who are you, beneath the cries
of wounded memories and bruised

hopes strung on rosaries and
hung sacrificial on crucifixes

Delving in depths kept secret
from mirror images and pretences for

your real face, your real name,
beyond martyrdom and conquest

KATHLEEN PANETTIERI

Universal child of stars and wild winds
and burning blinding suns

don't you know that an inalienable
infinity has breathed into you

and everywhere you look bleeds into
you, becoming who you are.

The anguish of Pierrot

There is danger
in each moment
I am drowning
in your eyes
And the moon
it does conspire
To keep me
hypnotised
Velvet night
the fiery light
Stars that chain me
to your empty heart
I stand here like
a clown in love
And sing to you
my mournful song
Pulcinella
Pulcinella

KATHLEEN PANETTIERI

There is magic
in each moment
I am drowning
in your eyes
But this magic
is just illusion
Like the cape of night
across the skies
Sweet Columbine
Cruel Columbine
You belong to
Harlequin
Bitter are these
tears I cry
Deep as night
this sea of sighs
Pulcinella
Pulcinella.

Epilogue

like a house
half empty
that someone
passed through
on some
yesterday
discarded
memories
that live
all alone
there
in a vacant
room
with walls
heavy and stained
with wistfulness
sometimes, a life
can be like this
a stolen kiss
a brief romance
full of
incompleteness
breath marks
left
on a misted window
a door
closed
on unfinished
things
un-said words

KATHLEEN PANETTIERI

stuck
in the throat
an after-thought
stranded
on a one-way
street
a backward
glance
no second
chance
a postscript
scribbled
on a racing
tailwind
no turning back
no turning back
sometimes, a life
can be like that.

Bazaar of abandoned things

Into a world of yesterdays
Where time has gone to sleep
Amongst dusty bric-a-brac
A lifeless doll no longer a playmate
Sits limp and stares vacantly
Clothes hang stiffly guarding a musty past
Discarded memories gaze
Wistfully into a misty future
I touch items that once were new
Now ready to spring into
Borrowed lives and mingle
With other tossed away memories
A deflated leather handbag
Zippered pockets
Empty and anonymous
Are a diary waiting to be filled
With the details of another woman's life
I weigh its worn softness on my arm
Pass burdened shelves and groaning tables
Their orphan whispers pleading
Pick me, choose me,
Give me another day
In the light of someone's life
I am not alone here, this place
Is a hub of busyness where others
Dip and delve as though
Someone else's life held
That piece missing from theirs

KATHLEEN PANETTIERI

I look for that one shining thing
To catch my eye and morph
From trash to treasure
I choose a tiny ornamental shoe
With a glittering golden trim
To walk out into the light with me.

Melancholy

The moon
Was in a sullen mood
Last night
She hid her face
Behind a cloud
One lonely star
Lit up the sky
While down below
The wolf hound howled
No lovers spooned
They stayed inside
Troubled was the moon
Her yellow face
She wanted to hide
I wonder
Does she ever get tired

Just hanging there
In all that space
Always crossing
The same old sky
Seen then hidden
In unbreakable rhythm

Sometimes, as I watch her
Climbing that sky
Night after night
Pulling and pushing me
With her tides, I feel
The strains of melancholy
That she possesses
Sisters, the moon and I,
Stains on our mirror of light.
Mysteries
Goddesses
Dragging our tides with us
Captives in our own vastness.

A street called one way

I'm holding you in a daze of exhaustion
A tiny stranger placed in my awkward unfamiliar arms
You don't seem quite real as you breathe and I hear you cry
I'm rocking your cradle in a haze of exhaustion
Hoping you won't cry anymore
I'm holding you as you take first steps
Steady now, I steady you hoping you won't fall
I'm watching you as you run away
I'm calling out and praying you listen
And come running back to the safety of my arms
I'm leaving you at the school gates
where time stretches away
Suddenly I'm waving to you as you drive away with bravado
I'm hearing you say "Yes, I will! " or No, I won't!"
I'm watching you grow away from me

Then I'm seeing your child take its first breath
I'm holding your child as I once held you
I'm watching a toddler run towards me laughing
I'm counting moments and tomorrows and years
I'm watching a child who looks just like you
Growing away from me because we are all wired to break free
Moving around like the sands that are never static
Running and running forward and away
Now, I'm older a little wiser and wearied by waves of exhaustion
The fire of my youth has burnt
its bridges

I know from time to time we will meet
On a street that is called one way
Where the ache in the bones of us lives
Breathe heart words like love and remember to each other
And for an infinitesimal moment
We will stop and stare backwards.

That primal cry

Out of the deepening throats of mutable winds
Can you hear the sobbing voices of violins?

I heard, I heard the cries of the children
All tangled in the branches of time

Dreaming of the fluttering of angels wings
Listening for their soft murmurings

Such yearning for enchanted things
From the depths of their cold, cold beds

Wooden crosses hanging like stigma
Over their innocent dreaming heads

Sweet lilting notes of the lullaby that once
Soothed the raw cry of birth

Drifting down now in fractured tones
To die upon the cold, cold earth

Time devouring in its sweeping streams
The stolen nebula of their fleeting dreams

Crushing them, one by one, back to dust
Like withered leaves off an endless tree

　　　　　　　　KATHLEEN PANETTIERI

I heard, I heard the sound of their voices
Echoing, still, that first primal cry
Do you feel, do you feel, do you feel
The sharp wounding bite of an ancient fear?

Can you see, can you see the falling rain
Pouring endless tears into their river of pain.

Firewall

Wake up, wake up
You're dreaming
Unscramble the wires
Of your tired brain
See the writing bleeding
In trails upon the wall
Wake up, wake up
You're dreaming
Only lies are needing
Protection
Break through
Your firewall

When the rains
Have turned to blood
And the ice
Becomes the flood
I am your worst nightmare
Come to wake you
From your sleep

When the rivers
Start crying
And the mountains
Are all dying
I am your worst nightmare
Come to wake you
From your sleep

When the sun
Has burned to coal
And its fire's
An ember of your soul
I am your worst nightmare
Come to wake you
From your sleep

When the lies
Have all been told
And you are
Left out in the cold
I am your worst nightmare
Come to wake you
From your sleep

When you lie
Naked on the ground
A waiting grave
All you ever found
I am your worst nightmare
Come to wake you
From your sleep

When the wind
Has blown away
The ashes that were
Here to stay

I am your worst nightmare
Come to wake you
From your sleep

Wake up, wake up
You're dreaming
Unscramble the wires
Of your tired brain
See the writing bleeding
In trails upon the wall
Wake up, wake up
You're dreaming
Only lies are needing
Protection
Break through
Your firewall.

KATHLEEN PANETTIERI

At the slip of your foot

The years are vengeful
They carry their grievances
Like the seasons
Rotating
Unchangeable
Each petty morsel
Chewed over and over
That will not be swallowed
Neither perfectly digested
Nor righteously released
Each bitter resentment
Each measured ounce
Of pitiful remorse
Measured and stirred
By turning tides
By avenging winds
That bluster and bite
At the running heels of time
Until one day
Inescapably
At the slip of your foot
They catch you
And crack you wide open
Spilling out
All the hidden things.

Deep pockets

There are days when the world
is a crying place
There are days when the world
is a dying place
And I feel like I am drowning
in its tears
And I am frozen in the ice
of its fears
Then I plunge my hands deep into the pockets of my soul
And feel the embers of life burning there
I see the light that has written a whole universe into being
And it is the light that is the source
of all seeing
So I look at the world from a different angle
And see a moving picture show with its play of shadow
Pulsing against an endless light
I tear off this mask of nihilism that
threatened to bring me down
Warm my hands in the burning embers of life
Tucked deep deep down in the
pockets of my soul
Feel the urgent and raw beauty of its pain
Let it spill its joy all over me again.

KATHLEEN PANETTIERI

Star crossed

I crossed the gypsy's palm
And watched as she
Shuffled her cards

Stacking them
Against me then
Casting them

Spiralling
To the sky
Then she read

My palm
And crossed me
With a lie

Fickle were the
The winds that blew
Dragging stars

From my eyes
Leaving love wounded
In a gypsy's palm

Tomorrow's secrets
Hidden jealously
In its hand

And the gypsy's
Words weaving a spell
Upon my mind.

Dreamers

Shadowy scrawls on subway walls
The melting candle wax that falls

Handprints of the ages petrified
Those ancient heroes we sanctified

Moments passing in puffs of smoke
Echoing words that once we spoke

Drifts of leaves falling from dancing trees
Now brush strokes on a passing breeze

Butterfly wings pinned to a bright blue sky
The trembling of our hearts, the questioning why

Our hungering souls hover at the edge of reality
Yearning for blessed moments of clarity

A plethora of yesterday
We reach out to grasp as it slips away

Those fleeting wings of time that flies
The aching lilt of old lullabies

Waking to find nothing as it seems
Just handfuls of dusty memories

Legions of the past knocking on heaven's door
The saints and the sinners who came before

KATHLEEN PANETTIERI

Were they real, did we just dream them all
Graffiti fading on a crumbling wall

Do you remember?
Who will remember?

The endless tolling of the bells that rang
The lingering pathos of that song we sang.

Earth dance

The ghost gum stands gaunt, solitary
Clinging to the side of its lone hill
Windswept, rainswept, eerily
Brushed by strands of moonlight
Its roots cling tightly to Mother earth
As mine do.
As the coastal cedars cluster
Gazing on the ocean, bathed
in its salty spray
As the tall oak blends into forests
Letting its old arms slowly bend
Acquiescent to the earth's pull
As the eucalyptus leans on mountain slopes
Sharing its scent with restless winds
And the desert palm stares across
lonely expanses
Feeling the bite of angry sands
I am like these trees, our roots
In the earth, our arms waving and
Dancing with the wind, moon and sun
Together we sustain each other.

KATHLEEN PANETTIERI

Ticket for the ride

Like a child again all brand new
Lining up in a jostling queue
Clutching my ticket for the ride
Candy floss dreams eager inside
Merry-go-round go round go round
Riding a horse with no feet on the ground
Up and down to a mechanical sound
Watching a world spinning by outside
Somebody switch off this crazy ride!
Merry-go-round go round go round

La rinascente

Let the wind
Take you where
It will
Your destination
A delicious
Mystery
Lightweight
Your baggage
Light-hearted
Your attitude
Willing to trust
The wind's
Direction
Willing to be
Reborn
Into the freedom
Of your spirit.

KATHLEEN PANETTIERI

KATHLEEN PANETTIERI

CPSIA information can be obtained
at www.ICGtesting.com
Printed in the USA
BVHW041609310821
615691BV00015B/470

9 780645 114560